WITHDRAWN

W9-BXL-815

Soup's On!

Soup's On!

Sixty Hearty Soups You Can Stand Your Spoon In

Janet Lembke

**Photographs by
William Nash and
Adrian C. Stanley**

THE LYONS PRESS

Guilford, Connecticut
An imprint of The Globe Pequot Press

For Wendy Hirsh, generous friend

The Lyons Press is an imprint of The Globe Pequot Press.

Printed in The United States of America

10 9 8 7 6 5 4 3 2 1

Library of Congress Cataloging-in-Publication Data is available on file.

Contents

Acknowledgments

To all of you who provided recipes for splendid soups, my heartiest thanks. No need to name you here, for your contributions are acknowledged with the recipes.

Then, many family members, friends, neighbors, and occasional passersby have helped in two ways to bring this book into being: taste-testing the products of my kitchen, and helping alleviate the refrigerator crisis that occurs when cooking on a massive scale is under way. They are Joe Kincaid, Laura Lembke, Lisa Tucker and Hamid Mazuji, Reta and Joe Nutt, Laura and David Stahl, and Ethel Smeak. I'm grateful for your comments and the fact that you all kept coming back for more.

My husband, the Chief, deserves commendation for putting up almost nonstop with the aromas of onions and garlic. Nick Lyons and my editor, Lilly Golden, are also to be thanked for their encouragement.

It's Soup!: An Introduction

Soup of the evening, beautiful Soup!
   —LEWIS CARROLL, *Alice's Adventures in Wonderland*

Soup also of the nooning, and the morning, too. Ever since people first discovered fire and cooking, they have in all likelihood used a word that sounds like *soup*. Soup, *soupe, sopa, zuppa, soep, Suppe*—say it in English, French, Spanish, Italian, Dutch, or German (which capitalizes its nouns), the word is basically the same. The fact that both the Romance and the Teutonic streams of Western language employ nearly identical terms for the stuff points to a shared ancestor in the far distant past. It also points to an ancient appreciation of ingredients mixed together and simmered in the various juices of plants and animals.

Soup is eclectic. It can be made of anything that's edible; it can be tailored for omnivores or vegetarians. And it's kind—babies and people needing dentures, as well as those in full possession of their teeth, find it palatable. Slurp and guzzle, down it goes.

My maternal grandmother, definitely not of the slurp-and-guzzle school, provided her grandchildren with a verse outlining the etiquette of eating soup: *As little ships go out to sea, I move my spoon away from me.* According to her, good manners also decreed that we sip wholly liquid soup from the side of a spoon, but for soups containing chunky ingredients, it was de rigueur to put the whole spoon into our mouths, silently close our lips around it, then withdraw the empty spoon. Under this system, a polite child was obliged to wait till the soup became lukewarm before taking the first bite. Today, every time I sit down to a steaming bowl of Chicken Noodle Picante or *Linsensuppe*, I think of her, even if I do occasionally slurp in order to cool it before it burns my tongue. To what extent the current generation heeds these rules, I cannot guess, but they're probably more honored in the breach than the observance.

For all my five decades as a cooking adult, soup has held a primary place in the meals prepared for family and friends. The kinds I like best are not dainty. They're meals-in-one; they're soups you can stand your spoon in. They fill the belly and stick to the ribs.

And the flavors—meat, seafood, garden vegetables, dried beans—taste like more. That is, it's hard to stop before the bowl is empty.

This book gives recipes for 60 favorites, along with how-to details on making soup stock, rather than relying on the canned supermarket versions. The instructions are both practical and irreverent, with absolutely no attention paid to such matters as calories and fat content. Most soups are lean by nature, unless there's been a heavy hand with oil or salt pork. The equipment needed is minimal. For making soup, I most often use a low and wide 5-quart Dutch oven, designated herein as "soup pot." For stock and soups that require more room, a tall, narrow 9-quart container—"stockpot" herein—comes into play. The tallness helps concentrate the flavor. The only other tools needed are a 2-quart saucepan, 12-inch skillet, blender, vegetable peeler, sharp paring knife, garlic press, stirring spoon, whisk, ladle, and a few bowls—bowls to hold ingredients, bowls to hold soup. The reason for the garlic press is that I find it easier to crush than to mince garlic cloves, which are slippery little devils.

Most of the recipes are easy to prepare, though some are time consuming. Only a few require specialty-store ingredients, but when something outré is called for, the address of a supplier is given, along with substitutes. Soup does not stand completely alone, of course. As a queen needs ladies-in-waiting, soup needs companions—sandwiches, salads, fruit, and, most particularly, bread or dumplings. Recipes for some of the last are included, along with occasional suggestions for the first three.

Most important, soup satisfies not only the flesh but also the spirit. I find as much pleasure in contemplating ingredients, their characteristics and intricate histories, as I do cooking and serving the products of my soup pot. And when it comes to the innate human urge for creativity, soup is an ideal medium. Take flings with ingredients, especially seasonings. Add cabbage, subtract eggplant, use red beans instead of white, go heavy on coriander but light on cilantro—almost anything goes.

Stir, simmer, and savor! And it's all right to slurp, at least a little. As the cowboy singer-comedian Smiley Burnette said in *Laramie Mountains*, a black-and-white western made in 1952, "Lots of good music in a bowl of soup—play a good tune with a *shloop, shloop, shloop.*"

Soup's
On!

Chapter One
The Lively Earth: Vegetable Soups

The word *vegetable* comes straight from a Latin word meaning "lively," "vigorous," and "brisk." Earth is indeed made quick by a wealth of plants—cabbages, onions, garlic, carrots, celery, eggplants, tomatoes, squashes, and their colorful, tasty compatriots. Satisfying both the palate and the eye, oh, how they enliven soup! Three of them—onion, carrot, and celery—might be called the canonical trinity of soup making, and two others, tomatoes and garlic, follow closely.

In my view, there's no such thing as too many onions—onions raw and onions cooked, onions fried and onions creamed, onions in the stew and onions in the soup. The plant, a member of the lily family, is formally known as *Allium cepa* or "garlic onion." The ancestral onion probably first grew in southwestern Asia but, from prehistoric times on, has spread around the world. The early Egyptians regarded the globe-shaped bulb as a symbol of the universe (so much for any flat-world theory). The Romans brought it to Britain, and European colonists introduced it into the New World. Through the millennia, onion lovers have sworn that the bulb was good for what ailed you; it was believed to cure colds, act as a diuretic, and make a poultice to heal the bite of a mad dog. There is one undeniable truth: As a 16th-century English botanist put it, "Onions are sharp, and move tears by the smell." As cooks know, they and their close cousin, the leek, also sweeten all that they simmer in.

Grated, diced, cut into strips or chunks, carrots also add a hint of sugar to the soup. It wasn't until the 19th century, however, that sweetness became a steadfast part of their taste. *Daucus carota*, or "carrot carrot" from its Greek and Latin names respectively, probably originated in two places: Europe for a white form of this member of the parsley family, and central Asia, where gardeners cultivated both a yellow and a violet form before the birth of Christ. But these two did not arrive in northwestern Europe until the 13th century. And it was only in the late 1600s that the carrot we now define by its orange color was developed in Holland from a cross between the yellow and violet sorts. Records from the time, however, describe its flavor as bitter or tart. Luckily, plantsmen persisted until they brought the underlying sweetness to the surface.

Celery, the third member of the trinity, is also a member of the parsley family, with the botanical name *Apium graveolens*, or "heavily scented parsley." A native of the Mediterranean, it was used in classical times as a flavoring. The Greeks also braided their celery, a plant with slender stalks and fine leaves, into crowns for the victors in the ancient Isthmian and Nemean games, which were equal in stature to those held at Olympia. The Roman naturalist Pliny wrote in the first century A.D. that celery juice was an antidote to the bite of venomous spiders. In the early 17th century, it was said to cure a host of other ailments, too, from canker sores and ulcers to agues. The lush, thick-stalked, leafy celery that we know was not developed until late in the 18th century. Hallelujah! As I chop and dice celery for soup, I also munch right then and there on a cool, crunchy greeny-white rib.

The tomato, a member (along with eggplant, potatoes, peppers, and tobacco) of the nightshade family, is almost as essential to soup as the trinity. Botanically, it's *Lycopersicon lycopersicum*, with each part of this double-barreled moniker meaning "edible wolf-peach." It received that name in the 18th century from men who seem to have thought that it was inferior to a true peach—a peach in wolf's clothing. The wild ancestral plant, which originated in Central and northern South America, bore tiny fruits resembling red currants. The common name we use today comes from Mexico, where the Spanish explorers picked up the Aztec word *tomatl*. The first report of tomatoes growing under cultivation in the United-States-to-be came in 1710, noting that they grew in the Carolinas, to which they had most likely been imported from the Caribbean. When it comes to tomatoes, my husband, the Chief, and I are fortunate: We grow all we need during the summer; I freeze and can pint after pint. When a recipe calls for diced or crushed tomatoes or tomato puree, I open a jar and transform its sweet red contents into the appropriate form.

And garlic—where would cooks be without garlic? Like the onion, it's a member of the lily family and the genus *Allium*. The whole name is *A. sativum*, "cultivated garlic." The plant originated in central Asia but grows wild also in Europe. And like the other vegetables that we've domesticated, it is said to work much magic, curing coughs, removing dandruff, countering the bites of venomous beasts, and keeping at bay all vampires and witches. Garlic's potency comes from the large helping of essential oils with which it is invested. Like onion, it sweetens as it cooks.

Here are recipes for soups with vegetables at heart—all, that is, except for beans and their kin, which warrant a chapter for themselves.

Old-Fashioned Vegetable Soup

With my husband, the Chief, I grow vegetables on a scale large enough to give us fresh produce in abundance during the summer and also to keep us in canned and frozen vegetables all winter long. This soup is the ideal medium, of course, for freshly picked peas, beans, corn, tomatoes, and other garden goodies, all filled with the tastes and aromas of sunshine and earth. But summer is evanescent, along with home-tended gardens and roadside stands. So ingredients found in the grocery store—cabbage, canned tomatoes, and frozen beans, peas, and corn—may be used to good effect. And don't forget leftovers. This soup also provides a handy-dandy way to use up those vegetable odds and ends that otherwise might migrate to the rear of the refrigerator. Leftovers have already been cooked, of course. So add them to the soup along with the cabbage, which cooks more quickly than the other ingredients.

Ingredients

4 cups vegetable or chicken stock (see pages 175 and179)

1 28-ounce can tomatoes (or 6 fresh tomatoes, peeled and chopped)

1 5½-ounce can V-8, or ¾ cup tomato sauce

1 large onion, diced

2 cloves garlic, pressed

1 carrot, diced

1 rib celery, diced

½ cup baby lima beans

½ cup cut green beans

½ cup peas

½ cup corn kernels

½ cup shredded cabbage

¼ cup macaroni alphabets

salt and pepper to taste

- Bring the stock, tomatoes, V-8, onion, and garlic to a boil. Reduce the heat and simmer, uncovered, for 10 minutes.

- Add the carrot, celery, limas, green beans, peas, and corn. Bring to a boil again. Reduce the heat and simmer for 20 minutes.

- Add the cabbage and alphabets. Simmer for 15 minutes. Season to taste, and ladle into bowls.

Serves 6.

Broccoli and Cheese Soup

My friend Sandy Taylor, a skilled calligrapher, is dark haired, bright eyed, and as southern as they come in regard to manners, drawl, and a certain mischievousness. She first came across the basics for her very special Broccoli and Cheese Soup in *Recipes from Miss Daisy's,* a cookbook from the mid-1970s that featured dishes from Daisy's Restaurant in Nashville, Tennessee. The restaurant, famous for its ladies' lunches, no longer exists. But you can't get anything approaching Sandy's soup in any restaurant. Since discovering Miss Daisy's version, she has experimented with it and doctored it to perfection. Her specific instructions are given below in quotation marks. When her version of the soup, gold with hints of green, is ready, she serves it with chicken or ham biscuits.

Broccoli—*Brassica oleracea* or "garden cabbage"—deserves a few words, too. It is botanically identical to cabbage, kale, cauliflower, brussels sprouts, and kohlrabi. They are distinguished one from another by group names. Cabbages, for one, are in the group Capitata, "forming heads." Broccoli's group is Italica, "from Italy," though it's really native to the Near East. But the Romans grew it in classical times, and its common name comes from Italy—"little sprouts," the plural diminutive of *brocco.* The wondrous variety of *B. oleracea* testifies ardently to the fact that human beings have been messing around with genetic engineering for a very long time.

This soup is wondrous, too, in flavor and richness.

Ingredients

2 cups water

2 chicken bouillon cubes

1 10-ounce package frozen broccoli florets or 1 pound fresh broccoli

1 large carrot, peeled and finely grated ("Do not leave out this secret ingredient.")

2 tablespoons butter

3 tablespoons flour

2 cups milk

2 pounds Velveeta cheese, broken into golf-ball-sized chunks

1 10¾-ounce can cream of chicken soup ("Cream of mushroom won't do.")

1 tablespoon minced onion flakes

2 tablespoons Worcestershire sauce

• Bring the water and bouillon cubes to a boil. Add the broccoli and carrot, and cook as directed on the broccoli package. Remove from the heat and reserve. Do not drain.

• Make a basic white sauce with the butter, flour, and milk in a large soup pot. Melt the butter on low heat. Add the flour and stir it in until well blended. Slowly add the milk, stirring constantly. When the sauce is medium thick, stir in the broccoli, carrot, and cooking water.

• Add the cheese, chicken soup, onion flakes, and Worcestershire sauce. Turn the heat to low and cook, uncovered, stirring frequently, until the cheese is thoroughly melted and all the ingredients have mingled and married.

Serves 6 to 8. Freezes well.

Spicy Cauliflower and Potato Soup

Like broccoli and cabbage, cauliflower is also *Brassica oleracea*. It is botanically distinguished from the others by its group name, Botrytis or "grapelike," which describes the tightly clustered flower buds. In an early feat of genetic engineering, cabbage that was bred specifically for its buds turned into cauliflower. Indeed, the common name comes from two Latin words, *caulis* and *flos,* that mean "cabbage" and "flower." Likely, it originated in China and gradually made its way west. The Moors brought it to Spain in the 12th century, but it did not reach Italy for another 200 years. It came to the New World with the earliest colonists. Thomas Jefferson grew it in his garden at Monticello; in February, we plant it in our garden in coastal North Carolina. Come May, true to the description of the poet Rita Dove, its heads shine "greenish-white in a light like the ocean's."

For me, one of the pleasures of this soup is being able to make it with the cauliflower that we harvested in spring, then put it into the freezer for use all year. The recipe is adapted from a fairly unimaginative one that appeared in a Wednesday food column in our local newspaper. For color, be sure to put red (not brown) potatoes and red (not green) hot peppers in the soup.

Ingredients

1 tablespoon olive oil

1 medium onion, chopped

3 large cloves garlic, chopped

2 medium red potatoes, unpeeled

1 16-ounce bag frozen or fresh cauliflower

1 4½-ounce can mild green chilies

1 fresh hot red pepper (jalapeño, chili, cayenne, your choice), seeded and minced

salt and pepper to taste

6 cups chicken stock (see page 179)

1 cup grated sharp cheddar cheese

- Heat the oil in a large soup pot. Add the onion and sauté, stirring occasionally, until translucent, about 5 minutes. Add the garlic.

- Meanwhile, cut the potatoes into 1-inch chunks. Add them to the pot. Cook for 10 minutes, stirring occasionally.

- Add the cauliflower, chilies, hot red pepper, salt, and pepper. Stir in the chicken stock. Bring to a boil. Reduce the heat, cover, and simmer for 15 minutes, until the potatoes and cauliflower are tender.

- Remove from the heat. Working in batches, blend until smooth. Return the puree to the pot. Bring to a boil, adding water if necessary. When the soup is hot, ladle it into bowls and garnish with cheddar cheese.

Serves 6.

Garlic and Leek Soup

Paul Repasy, New Hampshire resident and maker of handsome wooden signs, describes this soup as "one of the best soups for a garlic lover I've ever come across." Though the original inspiration came from a soup served at the Free Press, a restaurant in Portsmouth, New Hampshire, Paul has "fiddled with it"—his phrase—and made it his own. The recipe that he sent to me is decorated with pen-and-ink drawings of the two prime ingredients. The paprika is his touch, for he's Hungarian. He tells me that the Hungarian word for "soup" is not part of the soup-*soupe-zuppa* family. It's *leves* (pronounced LEV-esh, with a light accent on the first syllable). But soup by any other name tastes just as good, especially this one.

Warning: This soup seems very thick when it's cold. But please resist the temptation to add more liquid before you warm it up. Heat will thin it sufficiently.

Ingredients

10–12 large cloves garlic, unpeeled

3–4 medium leeks (white and pale green parts only), sliced into ½-inch rounds

2 tablespoons butter

½ cup diced salt pork

2 medium carrots, diced

3 ribs celery, finely diced

4 cups chicken stock (see page 179)

½ teaspoon paprika (mild or hot, as you prefer)

salt and pepper to taste

2 medium potatoes, peeled and diced

1 teaspoon fresh sage, finely chopped, or ¼ teaspoon dried sage (optional)

- Put the unpeeled garlic cloves on a wire rack (to help prevent scorching) and roast in an oven heated to 350° Fahrenheit for 25 minutes.

- Meanwhile, prepare the leeks, carrots, celery, and potatoes, with a separate bowl each for the leeks and potatoes (three bowls all together).

- When the garlic is roasted, peel the cloves. Melt the butter in a small saucepan over low heat, add the garlic, and mash with a fork to make a paste (which will look lumpy, but the lumps cook out). Set aside.

- Place the salt pork in a small saucepan with water to cover, bring to a boil, and cook for 3 minutes. Drain, place in a large soup pot, and cook over medium heat until golden, about 4 minutes. Discard all but 1 tablespoon of fat.

- Add the leeks. Cook for 1 minute, stirring constantly. Add the garlic paste. Cook for 1 more minute, stirring constantly. Add the carrots and celery, stir, reduce the heat, cover, and cook for 10 minutes, stirring occasionally, until the vegetables are tender.

- Stir in the chicken stock, paprika, salt, and pepper. Add the potatoes and bring to a boil. Reduce the heat, cover, and cook for 15 minutes, until the potatoes are tender.

- Puree at least 1 cup—more if you'd like—and return puree to the pot. Heat thoroughly and ladle into bowls. Garnish each bowl with a sprinkling of sage.

Serves 4. Does not take kindly to freezing, because of the potatoes.

Mushroom Soup with Barley and Pancetta

Mushrooms aren't members of the plant kingdom but claim a realm all their own, the fungi. But they, too, spring from the lively earth. A mushroom soup definitely deserves a place amid those that feature vegetables. And this one contains the three canonical vegetables—onions, carrots, and celery—along with garlic. The recipe here is my own, developed by experience and experiment.

It's highly amenable to adaptation:

- 1 cup of cooked brown rice may be put into the pot instead of barley. (The idea of brown rice as a thickener comes from my cousin Bess Nutt, a silversmith, who lives in New Hampshire and cooks a mean soup.)
- Use 2 large leeks or 4 shallots in place of the onion.
- Add tang with a crumbled, dried red pepper.
- Put a sprinkling of basil or thyme in the pot.
- Exercise your imagination.

Ingredients

2 tablespoons butter

1 pound golden-brown Italian mushrooms or button mushrooms, sliced thin

2 tablespoons flour

4 ounces pancetta or 4–6 slices bacon, cut into 1-inch pieces

1 large onion, diced

2 carrots, diced

2 ribs celery, diced

3 large cloves garlic, pressed

6 cups pork or chicken stock (see pages 180 and 179)

½ cup pearl barley

salt and pepper to taste

Parmesan cheese, freshly grated

- Melt the butter in a heavy skillet. Add the mushrooms and cook, stirring occasionally, until tender, about 10 minutes. Sprinkle the flour over the mushrooms and stir until thoroughly mixed, about 1 minute. Set aside.

- Meanwhile, put the pancetta in a large soup pot and fry over medium heat until crisp, about 6 minutes. (If you're using bacon, cook until crisp, then discard all but 1 tablespoon of the fat.)

- Add the onion, carrots, celery, and garlic to the pot. Mix them with the pancetta, cover, and cook, stirring occasionally, for 10 minutes, until the vegetables are tender.

- Stir in the mushrooms, mixing them thoroughly with the other ingredients. Add the stock and barley. Bring to a boil. Reduce the heat and simmer for 40 minutes, or until the barley is tender. Season to taste with salt and pepper. Ladle into bowls. Garnish with Parmesan cheese.

Serves 6. Freezes well.

Omnipotent Onion Soup

Patricia Moyer, teacher, poet, and excellent friend, was inspired by Henri de Toulouse-Lautrec (1864–1901) to create this soup. I learned from her that the painter was noted not only for his art but also for his cooking and gourmandizing. After his death, his longtime friend Maurice Joyant collected many of the recipes that he and Lautrec had prepared and savored. The result was *The Art of Cuisine*, a glorious compendium, which was translated into English and published in the United States in 1956, with the original metric instructions converted into tablespoons, cups, ounces, and pounds at the end of each recipe. The language is enchanting. The artist's recipe for *Soupe à l'Oignon* calls for "a laurel leaf and six or seven beautiful sliced onions." Along with recipes ranging from soups of many flavors to

"Grasshoppers Grilled in the Fashion of St. John the Baptist," Lautrec's drawings and paintings are sprinkled liberally, joyfully throughout. To our great good fortune, this grand book, though out of print, is readily available through dealers in used books. I found my copy through bibilofind.com.

Patricia's directions are as lively as Lautrec's. When she first told me about Omnipotent Onion Soup, she said this: "Take lots and lots of huge onions. Pounds and pounds. Slice them in great thick round slices. Cry away all your troubles as you do so. This soup requires a few tears being dropped into the pot to make it the most healing soup of the winter. Rinse your eyes with water, refreshed, restored, and begin cooking the onions. In lots of butter, slowly, slowly, turning with a wooden spoon often. Meditate on them until they turn yellowy, slightly, only slightly brown. Best if made just before new moon." Her preference is to use water instead of stock so that you do not "alter the true onion soup taste with carnivorous broths (delightful as they are for other soups)." She also suggests using a secret ingredient; one of her favorites is a tablespoon of medium curry powder. Cumin, basil, oregano, and a pinch of red pepper flakes are good possibilities, too.

Prime companions for this soup that Patricia deems "wondrous for certain sure" are a tossed salad with the dressing of your choice and a juicy piece of fresh fruit.

Note: Make this one in a large stockpot, not a 5-quart soup pot.

Ingredients

1/2 **pound butter**

3 **pounds onions, plus 1 more onion for luck, thickly sliced**

2 **cloves garlic, pressed (optional)**

8 **tablespoons whole wheat flour**

12 **cups water and/or stock (beef, ham, chicken)**

1 **tablespoon soy sauce**

Gruyère, Parmesan, or Swiss cheese, freshly grated

sliced, toasted bread

salt and pepper to taste

• Melt the butter in a large stockpot, and add the onions. Cook over low heat, stirring frequently, until onions soften in their own juices and begin— just begin—to turn brown, about 2 hours.

- Add the garlic. Then add the flour slowly, stirring constantly (or at least very frequently) for 15 minutes over low heat.

- Stir in 10 cups of the water and/or stock. Bring to a boil. Reduce the heat to low and simmer for 1 hour and 20 minutes.

- Top off with the remaining 2 cups water and/or stock, and add the soy sauce. Simmer for 2 hours and 40 minutes, until the soup is reduced by about half. Season to taste.

- For each serving, place grated cheese in the bottom of a deep oven-proof soup bowl. Ladle soup into the bowl. Cover each bowl with a slice of toasted bread. Add more cheese to cover the bread. Place the bowls in an oven heated to 350° Fahrenheit. Let the cheese melt, and serve.

Serves 6. Freezes well.

Potato Soup with Sour Cream

Cousins in the nightshade family to tomatoes, eggplant, and peppers, potatoes originated in the Andean highlands, and wild potatoes are still abundant in the Andes. When the Spanish conquistadores arrived, potatoes were widely cultivated in South America, from Chile to Colombia, though none were then grown farther north. North America received its potatoes in the 18th century from England, which had found them in Bermuda. The plant's scientific name pulls no punches but states precisely what it is: *Solanum tuberosum*, "nightshade full of tubers." The word *potato* itself is a transformation of *batata*, a Native American word used in Haiti to designate the sweet potato. It's easy, however, to see how the common name slid from one tuberous plant to another.

And, oh, the potato is splendid in soup, as one ingredient among many or all by itself, except for a bit of onion. As the main constituent of a soup, potatoes may be handled in several ways—mashing, blending, or whisking. I like the last, because it leaves small pieces of potato lurking in the liquid. The soup thickens overnight. So if you're not serving it right away, you may want to thin it a little with milk.

Ingredients

1 tablespoon butter

2 medium onions, diced

2½ pounds potatoes, peeled and sliced into ¼-inch rounds

6 cups chicken stock (see page 179)

1 bay leaf

8 ounces sour cream

salt and pepper to taste

scallions

- Melt the butter in a large soup pot over medium heat. Add the onions and cook until soft, about 3 minutes.

• Add the potatoes, stock, and bay leaf. Bring to a boil, then reduce the heat slightly and boil gently for 15 minutes, until potatoes are tender.

• Whisk the potatoes gently so that the soup thickens. There should be small bits of potato remaining in the pot. Slowly, a dollop at a time, whisk in the sour cream. Reduce the heat to low and let simmer for 10 minutes. Remove the bay leaf. Season to taste, ladle into bowls, and garnish with chopped scallions.

Serves 6. Do not freeze, for potatoes are unhappy with chilling temperatures.

Cream of Potato and Tomato Soup

Pat Schrishuhn, who lives in Danville, Illinois, is my younger son's stepmother-in-law. To put it more plainly, she is my son's wife's stepmother. But that information only identifies my connection with her. What really counts is that, when my son was an undergraduate at the University of Illinois, and not yet married to—only dating—the woman who is now his wife, he could not afford to come home for most holidays. I worried, of course, about how he was getting by and whether he was getting enough to eat. Well, not just enough, but with the right nutrients, as well. To my great maternal joy, I learned that Pat regularly and faithfully fed him—providing not only feasts on holidays but everyday fare as well. She's Polish, skilled in healthy, hearty cooking, and she has an affinity for food that satisfies the soul as well as the flesh. You'll meet her again in the minestrone department and in the bean and seafood sections of this book.

Pat found this cream of potato and tomato soup two or three decades ago in a catalog that interspersed recipes with ads for kitchen equipment and suppliers. (I suspect that the soup falls into the heirloom category, for the recipe Pat sent me specifies quantities in a most old-fashioned, decidedly British way—butter by the ounce, not the tablespoon; sugar by the lump, not the teaspoon.) She advises making the soup in summer, when real tomatoes, fresh from the garden, are available. But come winter, when the garden sleeps, the best, most flavorful supermarket choice is plum tomatoes, such as Roma. Pat also says that half of the success of this soup depends on the first step: "If the butter burns or leeks brown, the flavor will be spoilt." She adds, "This is an inexpensive and simple soup, in which you taste butter, cream, and each vegetable. It can be made thicker with the addition of extra potatoes." The recipe may also be easily doubled.

Ingredients

2 tablespoons butter

2 leeks (white part only), sliced fine

4 medium tomatoes or 6 plum tomatoes, peeled and coarsely chopped

2 medium potatoes

2 teaspoons sugar

pinch of salt

3 cups water

½ cup cream

1 tablespoon fresh chervil or parsley, chopped

• Melt the butter in a heavy soup pot over low heat. Add the leeks and let them soften in butter for about 4 minutes.

• Add the tomatoes and cook over medium-low heat until they release their juices. Stir in the potatoes, sugar, and salt, and cover with 3 cups of water. Simmer for 25 minutes, or until the potatoes are soft.

• Puree the soup in a blender and return it to the soup pot. Heat the cream to a boil, then whisk it into the soup. Stir in chervil or parsley just before ladling the soup into bowls.

Serves 3. Do not freeze.

Spinach Soup with Chickpeas and Potatoes

Because the flavor of this soup is beholden to spinach, rather than to chickpeas and potatoes, I place it in the chapter for vegetables, not that for beans and other legumes. Using frozen spinach, not fresh, and canned chickpeas rather than dried, it is a variation on a meal-in-one soup served in Spain during Lent. Frozen spinach is much easier to use, I think, than fresh, for the latter always seems to be grown in sandy soil and needs endless washings so that the soup is not salted with grit.

Both spinach and chickpeas warrant a few words about their provenance and history. The chickpea, *Cicer arietinum* or "chickpea that looks like a ram's head," is a legume indigenous to the Mediterranean and is known to have been cultivated as long ago as 7000 B.C. The Egyptians, however, did not recognize a ram in its appearance and called it "owl's head." The Latin word for chickpea is *cicero*, which served also as the family name of the Roman lawyer and orator Marcus Tullius Cicero. (Other Roman families also honored important food in their names: Fabius, or fava bean, and Lentulus, or lentil.) The chickpea has its own set of sobriquets; the one we know best is probably garbanzo, though elsewhere in the world, it's dubbed gram or Egyptian pea.

Compared to the chickpea, spinach, *Spinacea oleracea* or "garden spinach," is a come-lately. Its genus name comes from the Latin word *spinus*, "spine," and refers to the prickles on its seeds. A member of the goosefoot or beet family, it may have been anciently cultivated (Aristotle does mention its cousin chard), but the first mention of this plant native to the Mediterranean area came in A.D. 647, when the king of Nepal made a gift of spinach to the Chinese emperor. Since then, the history of spinach has included such notable fanciers as Albertus Magnus, Catherine de Medici, and Popeye.

The soup falls into the quick-and-easy category, taking no more than an hour to make.

> Ingredients
>
> 3 tablespoons olive oil
>
> I large onion, sliced thin
>
> 10 cloves garlic, chopped

6 cups chicken stock (see page 179)

2 large potatoes, peeled, cut in half lengthwise, and cut into 1/4-inch slices

1 15-ounce can chickpeas, drained and rinsed

1 10-ounce package frozen spinach, thawed and pressed dry

salt and pepper to taste

• Place the oil in a large soup pot over medium heat. Stir in the onion and garlic and cook until the onion becomes translucent. Add the chicken stock and potatoes. Bring to a boil. Reduce the heat and simmer for 30 minutes.

• Stir in the chickpeas and spinach. Simmer for 5 minutes, or until the chickpeas and spinach are heated through. Season to taste and ladle into bowls.

Serves 4. Do not freeze.

Butternut Squash Soup with Pancetta

From pumpkins to butternut, acorn, and Hubbard and on to crookneck and zucchini, the squashes are a New World phenomenon, no matter whether they're the hard-shelled winter kind or the soft-skinned squashes of summer. And of them all, butternut is by far the favorite at my house. This squash, rich gold in color, is naturally sweet in taste. We bake it with bacon or brown sugar. We mash it and eat it with much butter or convert the puree into butternut pie, butternut bread, and butternut soup.

Many soup recipes that specify butternut instruct you to peel, seed, and cut the squash into cubes, then simmer the cubes in stock until they soften. The next step is putting the squash and other ingredients into a blender. No, no, no! Two other methods of preparation are far more satisfactory.

- Bake it, after the skin has been lightly pricked, at 400° Fahrenheit for 1 hour. Let it cool. Remove the skin and seeds. Mash the pulp with a fork or potato masher.
- Cut the squash in half lengthwise, remove the seeds, and steam it, cut-side down, for 30 minutes, or until tender. Let cool. Remove the pulp from the skin and mash it.

The second method has the virtue of creating butternut stock. The liquid from steaming may be saved and used in the soup. And the mashed puree freezes very well indeed. In any season, I can go to my freezer rather than the supermarket.

As for pancetta, it's bacon, an uncured type of Italian provenance. Because it's not always easy to find outside metropolitan areas or communities, like college towns, that cater to international tastes, I have sometimes cooked this soup with fatty country ham bits. Lean ham of any sort can also be used, but put 2 tablespoons of olive oil in the pot so that the first four ingredients frizzle merrily.

Ingredients

4 ounces pancetta or country ham, coarsely chopped, or 4 ounces lean leftover

ham with 2 tablespoons olive oil

1 large onion, chopped

2 cloves garlic, pressed

¼ teaspoon red pepper flakes

7 cups stock (butternut, vegetable, chicken, or any combination of these stocks)

4 cups butternut squash, cooked and mashed as directed

1 large carrot, shredded

1 teaspoon cumin

½ teaspoon ground coriander

salt and pepper to taste

3/4 cup grated sharp cheddar (optional)

• Place the pancetta (or ham), onion, garlic, and pepper flakes in a large soup pot. Cook over medium-low heat, stirring frequently, until the onion is soft and translucent, about 10 minutes.

• Add the stock, butternut squash, carrot, cumin, and coriander. Bring to a boil. Cover and reduce the heat to a simmer. Cook for 45 minutes. Season to taste with salt and pepper. Ladle into bowls and, if desired, garnish each serving with grated cheddar.

Serves 6. Freezes well.

Grandma Smith's Tomato Soup

Grandma Smith's first name was Vesta, and she was a lifelong resident of Indiana. Given the stellar quality of this heirloom soup, which dates back at least as far as the early 1900s, it's fitting that she was named for the Roman goddess of home and hearth. I first met her soup when her daughter-in-law Gertrude Smith, also a lifelong Hoosier, stirred up a batch 10-plus years ago when she was visiting her son Al, our neighbor two doors down in coastal North Carolina. Gertie is a contagiously cheerful eighty-three-year-old woman. She and her husband, Dale, were wed at the DeKalb County Free Fall Fair in front of about 10,000 people, and when their 50th anniversary came around in 1987, that momentous occasion was celebrated at the fair. Theirs was a farm life, involving gardens and much putting up of food. The tomato is "good poetry," according to the poet Rita Dove, and this soup that I learned from Gertie and Al is good poetry to the last spoonful. It was so scrumptious on my first taste that I acquired the recipe then and there, went home, and stirred up a batch of my own. Gertie's recipe calls for "oleo" instead of butter, but she and her son Al think that Vesta used butter (which I prefer). Her recipe also specifies the use of 8 quarts of tomato juice, enough to make at least 16 pints of canned soup, with some left over for supper. I've cut the recipe in half, but it may certainly be doubled or halved again. It cans very well indeed, and I've used it not only as soup but also as an ingredient in French salad dressing. As I write, I'm listening to the *ping* of sealing jars.

The soup is naturally thick but may be thinned with milk or water. I keep it thick and gussy it up by adding 1 teaspoon dried basil and Tabasco sauce to taste. Then I indulge in a habit that my finicky grandmother would have deemed unacceptable—making a sandwich of American cheese and dipping it into the soup before each bite.

Note: Make the full recipe in a large stockpot. For a half recipe, a 5-quart soup pot will do.

Ingredients

½ cup water

1 cup diced celery

1 cup diced onion

½ cup thin-sliced carrot

4 quarts tomato juice

½ cup sugar

5 teaspoons salt

1 teaspoon chili powder

1 cup butter

1 cup flour

- Put the water, celery, onion, and carrot in a large saucepan, and cook over low heat until the carrot is tender, about 30 minutes. Drain and mash the cooked vegetables.

- Heat the tomato juice, sugar, salt, and chili powder to a boil. Add the vegetables and reduce the heat to a simmer.

- As this mixture simmers, melt the butter over low heat and stir the flour into it until it is smooth. (If you end up with lumps, they can be stirred out with a whisk.) Add this thickener to the juice-vegetable mixture. Bring to a boil. Can immediately in hot sterilized jars.

Makes at least 8 pints. Also freezes well.

Minestrone: Five Variations on a Theme

The word is Italian, the substance a soup of many colors. Minestrone is a thick, hearty vegetable soup that traditionally contains beans, rice or pasta, meat, and meat stock. Eaten with bread and wine, it comprises a noontime meal for "hungry working people," as the *London Sunday Times* has put it. And it comes in a motley host of variations, some specific to regions in Italy, some defined by their ingredients. Traditionally, it's the meat, from salt pork to slivers of Italian ham—prosciutto or pancetta—that makes the minestrone. If the soup comes solely from the garden, with its beans, tomatoes, and pasta simmered in tomato juice or vegetable broth, then it qualifies as *minestra.* That word also means "soup," and it's the old term from which *minestrone* was formed. Likely, it points to an earlier day in which meat was hard to come by, especially by those hungry workers mentioned above.

Two of the five recipes below qualify technically as meaty minestrone; the others are meatless minestra. They may, however, be gussied up with ham or cubed salt pork added at the time that broth or stock is mixed in. Likewise, the meat may be omitted from the Minestrone with Rice recipe. In all five, it's up to the cook to decide what kind of stock to use—vegetable, chicken, or beef. Water straight from the tap also works very well, for the vegetables provide sufficient flavor of their own.

All five are cooked uncovered or only partly covered. This lidlessness accounts for the thick quality of minestrone: Some of the liquid evaporates, leaving behind what amounts to a vegetable stew. Keep an eye on the liquid, and replace it as needed. More broth may be poured in, or water or tomato juice. One my favorite additives is V-8 juice.

Grace the soup when it's served with fresh-grated Parmesan and a dollop of olive oil. Italian bread, tossed salad, and fresh fruit—pears, apples—are fit companions for any one of this quintet. So is *Pan Relleno*—stuffed bread (page 193).

Minestrone is a soup that easily adapts to spur-of-the-moment inspirations. Each of the five is amenable to being enhanced by one or more of the following:

- any fresh or frozen leftover vegetables
- ½ teaspoon dried basil
- ½ teaspoon cumin
- ½ cup dry red wine
- ½-inch-thick Parmesan cheese rind, cooked directly in the soup

Minestrone with Rice

Two decades ago, I met this recipe as *minestrone di riso* when I worked as cook and general factotum in a palatial house in Princeton, New Jersey, in exchange for reduced rent while I taught a course in literary translation. The recipe makes nearly enough soup to feed a neighborhood. The Italian parsley specified is the flat-leaved kind readily found in supermarket produce sections. The Arborio rice called for may be found in specialty stores and many larger supermarkets. It can also be ordered over the Internet. But if it's not easily available, use ¾ cup long-grain (not instant) white rice. Cook it according to the instructions below, or add it to the soup pot along with the spinach, cabbage, tomatoes, and the whole 2 quarts of chicken stock. With the latter method, you'll need to add more liquid as the soup cooks. Save the juice from the drained tomatoes and beans to add to the pot along with more broth. As for the prosciutto or pancetta, which may not be easy to find, you may add an equivalent amount of just plain chopped ham to the pot.

Note: Make this one in a large stockpot, not a 5-quart soup pot.

Ingredients

8 ounces fresh spinach, washed and cut into strips, or 1 10-ounce package frozen spinach, thawed and drained

½ head cabbage, washed and cut into strips

3 tablespoons olive oil

8 sprigs Italian parsley, coarsely chopped

3 cloves garlic, chopped

2 ounces pancetta or prosciutto, coarsely chopped

1 small piece pancetta or prosciutto rind, coarsely chopped

2 ribs celery, cut into ½-inch pieces

1 carrot, cut into ½-inch pieces

1 medium red onion, coarsely diced

2 zucchini, cut into ½-inch pieces

1 medium potato, cut into ½-inch cubes

1 32-ounce can plum tomatoes, drained

2 quarts chicken stock (see page 179)

¾ cup Arborio rice

1 14½-ounce can kidney beans, drained

salt and pepper to taste

freshly grated Parmesan cheese

- Place the spinach and cabbage in a saucepan. Cover with salt and cook for 15 minutes. Squeeze dry and set aside.

- Place the oil, parsley, garlic, ham, and rind into a heavy stockpot and sauté gently for 15 minutes.

- Add the celery, carrot, onion, zucchini, and potato to the pot. Sauté for 5 minutes.

- Add the spinach, cabbage, tomatoes, and enough broth to cover (about 1½ quarts). Simmer for 40 minutes. Do not place a lid on the pot.

- Cook the rice in a mixture of boiling water and the remaining broth for 10 minutes. Drain and add to the soup for another 10 to 15 minutes. Add the beans. Season to taste. Serve with fresh-grated Parmesan.

Serves multitudes. Freezes, but with some loss of quality.

Eggplant Minestrone

Eggplant is glorious. With tomatoes, potatoes, and peppers, it's a member of the nightshade family, and it grew first in India but was taken early on to China and the Near East. Botanists call it *Solanum melongena,* "mad-apple nightshade," a name that reflects a long-standing suspicion in northern Europe that it could poison and perhaps kill anyone who took a bite. In the late 16th century, an English herbalist had this to say of it: "It is better to esteem this plant and have him in the Garden for your pleasure and the rareness therefore, than for any virtue or good qualities yet known." Thank goodness that we know better now. But what do you do when the garden bursts and presents you with eight glossy, night-purple eggplants all at once? Give some to the neighbors, of course. Make soup from the rest.

This soup is an excellent candidate for being fancified:

- Add diced bits of bell pepper, fresh limas, or both.
- Throw in ½ teaspoon cumin.
- Use tomato juice combined with chicken broth as the basic stock. When it comes to putting more liquid in the pot, don't scant on the V-8. Wine works, too—½ cup, red or white.
- And if you're not a dried-bean fan, use 1 14½-ounce can dark red kidney beans, undrained; add them at the last minute and let them simmer only until they're heated through.

Ingredients

¼ cup dried beans, white or red

2 tablespoons olive oil

1 large onion, chopped

3 cloves garlic, minced

1 medium eggplant, peeled and diced into ½-inch cubes

2 small zucchini or yellow crookneck squash, sliced in ⅛-inch rounds

2 carrots, peeled and sliced into ⅛-inch rounds

2 ribs celery, diced

8 large tomatoes, peeled and quartered, or 2 14 ½ -ounce cans tomatoes, undrained

4 cups vegetable stock (see page 175)

½ cup dry red wine

1 teaspoon dried oregano

1 teaspoon dried basil

1 teaspoon salt

1 teaspoon sugar

½ cup small pasta shells or ditalini

¼ teaspoon pepper

- Soak the beans overnight in water to cover. Drain and reserve.
- Place the olive oil, onion, and garlic in a large soup pot.
Sauté for 5 minutes.
- Add the eggplant to the pot and cook for 3 minutes, stirring frequently.
- Add the squash, carrots, celery, tomatoes, beans, vegetable stock, wine, oregano, basil, salt, and sugar to the mixture. Simmer, uncovered, for 1 to 2 hours. Add more broth as necessary.
- Add the pasta and pepper. Cook for 30 minutes. Ladle into bowls.

Serves 8. Freezes well.

Minestrone with Meatballs

Here's a version of minestrone from Pat Schrishuhn, who saved my younger son from starvation in his college days. She thinks that the recipe originated long ago in the *Chicago Tribune*. Wherever it came from, it is delicious. I recommend making a double batch of the meatballs so that half of them go into the soup and half into the freezer, where they'll last nicely until you need them for this minestrone or another soup like Lucky 13-Bean Soup (page 60).

Ingredients

For the meatballs:

1 tablespoon olive oil

8-ounce mixture of ground veal and beef

2 tablespoons finely chopped, onion

1 garlic clove, chopped

2 tablespoons Italian bread crumbs

1 egg yolk

pinch each of dried basil, oregano, parsley, salt, and pepper

For the soup:

1 14½ -ounce can kidney beans

¼ cup chopped celery

¼ cup shredded cabbage

3 tablespoons chopped onion

1 garlic clove, chopped

2 tablespoons olive oil

2 cups beef broth (see page 177)

1 14½-ounce can Italian tomatoes

1 bay leaf

1 clove

salt and pepper to taste

freshly grated Parmesan cheese

• Mix the meat, onion, garlic, bread crumbs, egg yolk, and various pinches into a stiff paste. Shape into olive-sized balls, brown in oil, remove from the pan, and set aside.

• Drain and rinse the kidney beans. Set aside.

• Place the celery, cabbage, onion, garlic, and oil in a soup pot and sauté for 5 minutes.

• Stir in the beef broth and tomatoes. Bring the mixture to a boil, reduce the heat, and simmer for 20 minutes.

• Add the meatballs, beans, bay leaf, and clove. Simmer for 10 minutes. Season. Sprinkle each serving with 1 teaspoon freshly grated Parmesan cheese.

Serves 4. Freezes well.

Hearty Tuscan Minestrone

The recipe below first appeared in the local paper. Bursting with tomatoes, beans, and spinach, it seemed Italian in its provenance. Indeed, the spinach makes it Florentine. But that newspaper recipe called for an exotic pasta that I'm sure never graced any *zuppa* indigenous to Italy: pierogi, also called piroshki. They are the dough-encased meat patties that traditionally accompany Russian soup. The first time I prepared this Tuscan delight, I discovered that the pierogi overwhelmed the other ingredients; they floated amid the broth and vegetables like great, pallid lumps. The next time around, it was out with the pierogi and in with truly Italian tortelloni or potato gnocchi. It can also be made with potato dumplings (page 195). I've since taken it to various writing workshops as my share of the potluck. Never has any been left to bring home.

Ingredients

2 teaspoons olive oil

1 large onion, finely diced

6 cups chicken stock (see page 179)

1 14½-ounce can Italian stewed tomatoes

1 9-ounce package cheese- or mushroom-filled tortelloni, or 8 ounces potato gnocchi

1 14½-ounce can red kidney beans, rinsed and drained

1 10-ounce package chopped frozen spinach, thawed and excess water pressed out

1½ teaspoon garlic powder

½ teaspoon dried basil

½ teaspoon dried oregano

freshly grated Parmesan cheese

• Heat the oil in a large soup pot over medium heat. Add the onion and cook and stir until tender, about 3 minutes.

- Add the broth and tomatoes. Bring to a boil. Add the tortelloni or gnocchi and cook according to package directions (about 4 minutes for tortelloni, 3 to 4 minutes for gnocchi). Add the beans, spinach, garlic powder, basil, and oregano. Cover and simmer until the spinach is tender, about 1 minute. Ladle into bowls and sprinkle with Parmesan cheese.

Serves 6. Freezes well.

Harvest Minestrone

The recipe for Harvest Minestrone comes from Donna Lewis, a friend living near Richmond, Virginia, who is not only a skilled painter of landscapes but also a superb cook of vegetarian soups. This soup is best made in summer with vegetables fresh from the garden or roadside stand. For wintertime cooking (or when the supermarket produce is limp and unappetizing), frozen green beans and corn will suffice. If you use frozen veggies, add them to the soup at the same time as the tomatoes, squash, and kidney beans.

Variation: Potato dumplings (see page 195) give an extra heartiness to this good soup.

Ingredients

1 large onion, diced

1 rib celery, diced

2 cloves garlic, chopped

1 large carrot, diced

½ cup fresh green beans cut into ½-inch pieces

½ cup fresh corn kernels

6 cups vegetable stock (see page 175)

3 large tomatoes, peeled, seeded, and chopped

1 small yellow crookneck squash, cut into ⅛-inch rounds and quartered

1 small zucchini, cut into ⅛-inch rounds and quartered

1 medium potato, peeled and cut into ½-inch cubes

½ cup canned kidney beans

• Put the onion, celery, garlic, carrots, green beans, corn, and 1 cup of the vegetable stock in a large soup pot. Cook, covered, over medium-high heat for 5 minutes.

• Add the remaining stock, tomatoes, squashes, and kidney beans. Bring to a boil. Reduce heat and simmer, partly covered, for 30 minutes.

Serves 6.

Tunisian Vegetable Stew

Donna Lewis first met this recipe in an old issue of *Vegetarian Life*. I first met it at her house, when she was living in North Carolina on Broad Creek, a tributary of the wide and salty River Neuse. The light sparkled on the water. Closer at hand, birds—cardinals, chickadees, titmice, and red-winged blackbirds—visited the feeders on the deck. Inside, her little Welsh terrier Duffy at our feet, Donna and I sat at the table watching the bird circus, talking a blue streak, and eating this fine vegetable soup. With it, she served crusty Italian bread. As for Tunis, the spices are typical of those used in North African cuisine. Turmeric, however, originated in India, where its bright orange powder, made from the dried rhizome of a perennial plant, has been used immemorially for its own earthy taste, as an ingredient of curry powder, and as a dye that imparts a saffron color to the robes of Buddhist monks.

Hallelujah for imported soups like this one! It's quick and easy to prepare.

Ingredients

2 tablespoons olive oil

1½ cups sliced onion

3 cups shredded cabbage

salt to taste

1 large green bell pepper, coarsely diced

2 teaspoons ground coriander

½ teaspoon turmeric

½ teaspoon cinnamon

cayenne to taste

1 28-ounce can tomatoes, undrained and chopped

1 15-ounce can chickpeas, drained and rinsed

⅓ cup raisins or dried currants

1 tablespoon fresh lemon juice

feta cheese, crumbled

toasted slivered almonds

- Heat the oil in a large soup pot. Add the onion and sauté until translucent, about 6 minutes.

- Add cabbage, sprinkle with a dash of salt, and sauté for 5 minutes.

- Add the bell pepper, coriander, turmeric, cinnamon, and cayenne, and mix together thoroughly.

- Stir in the tomatoes, chickpeas, and raisins or currants. Simmer for 20 minutes until the vegetables are tender. Add the lemon juice. Ladle into bowls and garnish with feta cheese and almonds.

Serves 4.

Very Veggie *Zuppa*

Hazel Dawkins, born and brought up in England and still much in possession of a posh accent, has resided in the United States for decades. Living in suburban Philadelphia, she works as a self-employed editor and writer—and she cooks. Of this soup, she says, "I created it because I'm nuts about carrots." You'll note also that it has decidedly Far Eastern leanings—soy sauce, Oriental noodles, and tofu. The last ingredient makes this soup splendidly nutritious, for tofu, made from soybeans, is packed with protein. And I cannot refrain from commenting on the soup's vibrant color—a rich carrot orange, of course, that's highlighted by the dark green of broccoli. Hazel's comments are given in quotation marks below.

Note: Make this one in a large stockpot, not a 5-quart soup pot.

Ingredients

¼ cup olive oil

2 (or more) large onions, chopped

2 pounds carrots, peeled and "sliced any way you want"

1 large sweet potato, peeled and cut into 1½-inch chunks

6 cups water

juice of 1 lemon

1 teaspoon soy sauce

salt and pepper to taste

"handful of broccoli" (1 to 1–1½ cups florets)

2 ribs celery, finely diced

1 cup Japanese or Chinese noodles, cooked

1 8-ounce cake firm tofu, chopped into squares

- Heat the oil in a large stockpot. Add the onions and sauté until transparent.

- Remove from the heat. Add the carrots, sweet potato, and water. Cover and bring to a boil, then reduce the heat to a simmer and cook for 30 minutes, until carrots are tender. ("Watch it doesn't boil over; if necessary, the lid can be partially tilted. The aim is to keep the liquid in the pot, not escaping as steam.")

- Remove the pot from the heat. Working in batches, blend the ingredients. ("Now you have created your basic stock.") Return the puree to the pot.

- Add the lemon juice, soy sauce, and salt and pepper. ("Hey, stop sipping it. Save some for the meal!")

- Stir in the broccoli florets and celery. Bring to a boil. Reduce the heat and cook, uncovered, until the florets and celery are tender, about 30 minutes. Add the noodles and heat just long enough to warm them, about 1 minute. "Just before serving, add tofu squares so that they are gently warmed."

Serves 8.

Chapter Two
Full of Beans, Peas, and Other Legumes

The legumes are a fabulous family, in all their delicious multiplicity: New World green and shell beans and Old World fava beans, along with lentils, peas, and those plants bearing *pea* in their names—chickpeas and black-eyed peas—that occupy botanical niches of their own. The word *legume* comes from the Latin verb *legere,* "to gather," and it speaks of the ease with which the seeds of leguminous plants may be collected.

In classical times, the Greeks and Romans believed that beans were magical. Pythagoras, well known for his famous theorem about the sum of the squares of the legs of a right triangle equaling the square of the hypotenuse, believed that beans gave the souls of the dead their passage to the hereafter. The Roman naturalist Pliny honored beans for their many practical uses: plain good eating at the table, mixed with grains and used as flour for bread, or stewed as an offering to the gods. He also assured his readers that those who carried a bean home from the harvest would have good luck.

I agree that beans are magical, but most especially in soup.

Legions of soup recipes call for beans and their cousins, and sometimes for several different legumes in the same pot. Here's a baker's dozen of my favorites.

Bean Soups

Beans, beans, they're good for your heart. The more you eat, et cetera. So begins the unseemly ditty that my children brought back from junior high school. As it happens, beans are literally good for the heart and the rest of the body, too: They're an excellent source of protein and fiber. Fresh or dried, they come in numerous guises. Fava or broad beans originated in the Old World; you'll find these wide, flat beans under the name *Italian beans* amid the supermarket's frozen foods. The other beans come from the New World, long used by Native inhabitants, then discovered and transported to Europe by the Spanish conquistadores (who often clanked in full armor over uncharted hills and dales). Red, kidney, black, navy, pinto, cranberry, cannellini, and lima beans—we know them by many names, but they are all, except for limas, botanically *Phaseolus vulgaris,* which is Greek for "bean" and Latin for "common." How can so many colors and flavors come from one and the same source? Think of the variety within a human family that shares an identical gene pool; it may contain redheads, brunettes, and blondes, both blue eyed and brown eyed, plump and lean, and further distinguished one from another in variants of body and personality. So it is with the New World beans, a grand group that also includes green beans, wax beans, and scarlet runners in a boggling number of varieties. The lima, a New World bean originating in South America, is *P. limensis,* a name that points to its first home.

Many of my recipes for bean soup call for dried beans. But see the tips below:

Tip 1:   Canned kidney beans and limas can often be substituted for their dried counterparts. Proportions are given in the recipes.

Tip 2:   Some dried beans and other legumes can be cooked without being soaked first. Limas are the eternal exception; even with soaking they can be mighty chewy. But to be on the safe side, it's a good idea to immerse any and all beans using one of two methods:

Cold: Place beans in a large bowl, cover with at least 3 inches water, and let sit overnight in the refrigerator. Then drain and rinse in cold water before placing them in the soup pot.

Hot: Place beans in a soup pot, cover with 2 inches water, bring to a boil, and cook for 2 minutes. Remove from the heat, and let soak for 2 hours. Then, as with cold soaking, drain and rinse in cold water.

Chief's Navy Bean Soup

My husband, a retired navy man whom I call the Chief, expressed a desire—no, a craving—for navy bean soup not long after we married. So I experimented, combining the essential navy beans with all sorts of ingredients. He gobbled down most of the experiments but informed me that they weren't navy bean soup, especially not the version with tomatoes. I finally came up with something that fancifies the dish that the navy's cooks prepared. They used just beans—with no other vegetables—and always served it at lunch, along with bread and salad. But the Chief has not complained since the version given below was first ladled into his bowl.

Navy beans do not need presoaking. The liquid and the heat of cooking soften them nicely. When the soup is done, I serve it up with grilled Edam or Gouda cheese sandwiches and applesauce, which is said to be an antidote for the Bean Problem alluded to in a well-known ditty: Beans, beans, the musical fruit. The more you eat the more you toot. The more you toot, the better you feel. So eat your beans at every meal.

Ingredients

2 cups navy beans

2 quarts ham stock (see page 180), or 2 quarts water with 1 beef bouillon cube

¼ pound lean salt pork, cubed

⅛ teaspoon pepper, freshly ground

¼ teaspoon garlic powder

¼ teaspoon dried marjoram

1 large onion, diced

1 rib celery, diced

1 potato, peeled and cut into small cubes

salt to taste

• Put the navy beans, stock (or water), salt pork, pepper, garlic powder, and marjoram into a large soup pot. Bring to a boil, then reduce the heat and simmer for 2 hours.

• Add the onion, celery, and potato. Continue simmering for 1 hour more. Add salt to taste. Serve.

Serves 6. Freezes well.

Bean Soup à la Deluxe Restaurant

The Deluxe Restaurant, a dining place founded in 1935, is located in Danville, Illinois. Danville is also the home of Pat Schrishuhn, soup cook supreme and stepmother-in-law to my younger son. Pat gave me the restaurant's recipe, which I suspect is an heirloom because it does not give exact proportions for all the ingredients but calls for "garlic, small amount" and simply "chopped ham." It also specifies using a No. 2 can of tomato juice. But years have passed since the sizes of cans were determined by numbers; today, they are measured in ounces, at least in the United States. So I've experimented with proportions here and come up with a virtual Deluxe Restaurant soup, not exactly the same but so close as makes no never mind.

Note: Make this one in a large stockpot, not a 5-quart soup pot.

Ingredients

2 cups dried white beans (great northern or navy), or 1 14½-ounce can,
 rinsed and drained

8 cups ham stock (see page 180)

1 cup diced onions (1 large onion)

1 cup diced celery (2 large ribs)

1 green bell pepper, diced

2 cloves garlic, pressed

1 11½-ounce can tomato juice

1 10¾-ounce can tomato puree

2 tablespoons sugar

2 cups cooked ham, cut into ¼-inch cubes

salt and pepper to taste

- Place the beans and ham stock in a large soup pot and bring to a boil. Reduce the heat and simmer, covered, until the beans are tender (Pat's recipe says "until soupy"), about 2 hours.

- Add the onion, celery, green pepper, garlic, tomato juice, tomato puree, and sugar. Simmer until tender, about 1 hour.

- Add the ham, and simmer just long enough for the ham to heat through. Season to taste and ladle into bowls.

Serves 8. Freezes well.

Pasta e Fagioli

There are as many recipes for *Pasta e Fagioli*, the quintessential Italian pasta and bean soup, as there are stars in the firmament. And depending on the book that you consult, you'll be told that the recipe is indigenous to regions as far apart as Sicily and the Veneto, in which Venice is located. Some recipes sternly specify white beans and white only, such as navy beans or cannellini, while others call for pinto or cranberry beans. The choice is yours and may well involve a combination of two or three types. As for the liquid, I use water, though chicken or beef stock is certainly acceptable. My water, however, is beany, for I use the stuff in which the beans were soaked overnight. But wash the beans before soaking if you want to use that liquid.

Pasta e Fagioli welcomes adaptations. Here are some that you may want to try:

- A dash of rosemary, a hint of cumin, a smidgen of fennel seed.
- A rind of Parmesan cheese, 1 inch thick. As with minestrone, this soup gains savor if the rind is added to the soup at the same time that the dry pasta is stirred in. The cheese will dissolve as the soup simmers.
- 1 crumbled cayenne pepper or ½ teaspoon dried red pepper flakes.

Note: Make this one in a large stockpot, not a 5-quart soup pot.

Ingredients

2 cups dried beans

8 cups water, including soaking water

2 tablespoons olive oil

1 large onion, finely diced

6 cloves garlic, pressed

1 rib celery with light yellow-green leaves, diced

1 28-ounce can diced tomatoes

½ cup dry white wine

½ teaspoon dried basil

¼ teaspoon dried oregano

1 cup small pasta shells, tubetti, or ditalini

salt and pepper to taste

olive oil, freshly grated Parmesan cheese, and finely chopped parsley (for garnish)

- Cover the beans with 2 inches of water and let them soak overnight. Drain, reserving the liquid.

- Place the water and beans in a large soup pot. Bring to a boil. Reduce the heat and simmer, partially covered, for 1 hour, until the beans are tender.

- Meanwhile, heat the oil in a large skillet over medium-low heat. Add the onion and sauté until translucent, about 3 minutes. Add the garlic and celery, and sauté for 2 more minutes. Stir in the tomatoes and their juices. Bring to a boil. Reduce the heat and simmer for 15 minutes.

- Working in batches, puree half of the beans in their liquid. Return them to the pot.

- Stir in the onion, garlic, celery, and tomato mixture. Add the wine, basil, and oregano. Bring to a boil. Add the pasta. Lower the heat slightly and cook at a gentle boil for 8 minutes, stirring frequently, until pasta is tender.

- Season to taste and ladle into bowls. Garnish each with a drizzle of oil, 1 tablespoon freshly grated Parmesan, and 1 tablespoon parsley.

Serves 8. Freezes well.

Chill-Chaser Bean Soup

This one brings warmth to body and spirit—just right for winter's most frigid weather. It's my favorite version of a soup that calls for more than one variety of bean. White beans, red beans, black beans—any and all of them will do, and don't forget limas. Nor do I stick with beans alone; I often add split peas and lentils to the hodgepodge.

For a variation, use 1 28-ounce can of Italian-style stewed tomatoes, with diced green bell peppers and a dash of basil and oregano, instead of plain tomatoes. Then instead of 2 quarts water, use 1 quart water and 1 quart tomato juice.

Ingredients

2 cups mixed dried beans (5 or more varieties)

2 tablespoons salt

2 quarts water

2 cups diced ham or sliced smoked sausage

1 large onion, chopped

1 clove garlic, pressed

1 teaspoon chili powder

1 28-ounce can tomatoes, chopped

1–2 tablespoons lemon juice

salt and pepper to taste

- Rinse the beans and place them in a large soup pot. Cover with 3 inches of water, add the salt, and let them soak overnight.
- Drain the beans and return them to the pot. Add 2 quarts water and the ham or sausage. Bring to a boil. Reduce the heat and simmer for 2 ½ to 3 hours.
- Add the onion, garlic, chili powder, tomatoes, and lemon juice. Simmer for 45 minutes. Season to taste and serve.

Serves 6.

Lucky 13-Bean Soup

Linda Hasselstrom, who lives in Cheyenne, Wyoming, or on her ranch in South Dakota, and writes eloquent, sometimes heartrending essays and poems about life in the West, developed this recipe with her partner, Jerry Ellerman, as a soup mix for Christmas giving. They packaged the beans and spices in a quart Mason jar and tied a tiny bottle of Tabasco sauce in the bow. Not all the beans are actually beans. Although any combination of 13 beans and other dried ingredients will do, Linda and Jerry use black-eyed peas, green and yellow split peas, lentils, pearl barley, bulgur wheat, and these beans: black, anasazi, baby lima, red, navy, pinto, and garbanzo. They also offer a grand array of variations on the basic soup:

- Add a can of tomatoes, tomato paste or sauce, or leftover vegetables.
- Add almost any meat, including sausage, hot dogs ("Bleah!" says Linda), bacon, or leftover meats, especially ham.
- Add 1 to 2 tablespoons chili powder, cumin, oregano, or other spice.
- Put in a handful or two of pasta 10 minutes before serving.
- Add red pepper flakes, salt, and pepper to taste, along with Tabasco sauce.

Linda's comments on the ingredients and the instructions below are enclosed in quotation marks.

Note: Make this one in a large stockpot, not a 5-quart soup pot.

Ingredients

4 cups any combination of available beans and other dried ingredients

8 cups water

1 bay leaf (If you present a jar of beans and spices as a gift,

"It will keep the beans free from crawlies for at least a year.")

1 tablespoon onion flakes, or 1 onion, chopped

1 teaspoon garlic powder, or 2 cloves garlic, chopped

½ teaspoon paprika

¼ teaspoon dried savory

½ teaspoon dry mustard

½ teaspoon dried basil

Tabasco sauce to taste

- "Dump the beans into a colander and wash. Cover with water and soak overnight."

- "Pour 1 glass of your favorite wine or beer. Sip slowly as you follow the instructions. Drain the beans." Place the beans and water in a large soup pot. Simmer slowly, covered, until tender, about 2 hours.

- If you'd savor a thicker soup, take some of the beans out at this point, puree them, and return them to the pot.

- Add the seasonings, including the bay leaf. "But don't eat it. Bay is good luck as seasoning, very bad luck if eaten." Choose, if you like, from the options given above. "Dump in some of whatever you're drinking, unless it's milk."

- Simmer for 20 to 45 minutes longer. "Serve with French bread, crackers, and a green salad. Sprinkle with Tabasco sauce to taste. Or top with shredded cheese."

Serves 6. Freezes well.

Black Bean Soups

Black beans, the *frijoles negros* that are a quintessential part of Mexican cuisine, have a uniquely nutty flavor. Though navy, pinto, kidney, cannellini, cranberry, and any other varieties are genetically identical and often taste much like one another, any soup made with black beans can be identified—no need to see it—by tongue alone. Nor is there just one kind of black bean soup. They may be prepared in a wide range of heats—from none at all (like the stuff in the Campbell's can) through mild and medium to five-alarm fiery. I offer two versions here. The first, with whole beans, is on the mild side. The second has bite.

Essential to both is cumin, an ancient spice native to the eastern Mediterranean and the Near East. It is listed in the inventory of commodities on the Linear B tablets found at Mycenae in Greece—written testimony to its importance in the 14th century B.C. Ten centuries later, Theophrastus, a Greek philosopher and naturalist, described it this way: "Cumin has the most fruits of any plant. There is an odd thing that is said of it: when people are sowing it, they must curse and slander it if they want it to be healthy and prolific." Now, there's a fine excuse for using bad language! But it surely adds an excellent touch of flavor to black bean soup.

Mild Black Bean Soup

This one may be prepared with either dried or canned beans, which are left whole rather than being put through a blender. It is the fruit of experimentation with a slew of recipes. I combined the best from each—carrots here, tomato paste and cumin there—to come up with an agreeable medley.

Ingredients

2 cups dried black beans, or 1 14½-ounce can, drained and rinsed

2 tablespoons olive oil

1 large onion, diced

1 rib celery, chopped

1 small carrot, grated

1 6-ounce can tomato paste

1 tablespoon ground cumin

2 quarts beef stock, (see page 177) or canned beef broth

juice of 1 lemon

salt and pepper to taste

• If you're using dried beans, put them in a large bowl and soak them using one of the two methods described on page 51. Drain and rinse them in cold water. Reserve.

• Heat the oil in a large soup pot over medium-high heat. Sauté the onion, celery, and carrot until tender, about 8 minutes. Add the tomato paste and cumin. Reduce the heat to medium and cook for 10 minutes, stirring frequently.

• Add the beans and stock. Cover and simmer for about 2 hours, stirring occasionally, until the beans are tender. (If you're using canned beans, simmer for only 30 minutes.) Add the lemon juice. Season to taste with salt and pepper.

Serves 6.

Spicy Black Bean Soup

Pat Schrishuhn, who has provided recipes for Minestrone with Meatballs (page 39) and Bean Soup à la Deluxe Restaurant (page 54), is one of the best soup cooks I know. Here she provides instructions for a black bean soup with heat—hot-pepper heat. It may be tamed or given greater bite, depending on the quantity of peppers and the kind of salsa. I like it hot—and have the pleasure of using cayenne peppers that were grown in our garden, then harvested and dried.

Ingredients

2 tablespoons vegetable oil

⅔ cup diced onion

4 cloves garlic, pressed

1 tablespoon cumin

½–1 teaspoon red pepper flakes

1 14½-ounce can chicken broth

3 15½-ounce cans black beans, undrained

3 cups thick and chunky salsa, mild or medium

2 tablespoons fresh lime juice

½ cup plain yogurt or sour cream

• Put the oil, onion, garlic, cumin, and red pepper flakes in a large soup pot, and sauté over medium heat until the onions are translucent, about 5 minutes. Remove from the heat.

• Working in batches, puree the chicken broth and 2 cans of undrained beans in a blender. Add to the pot. Stir in the remaining can of beans along with the salsa and lime juice.

- Heat the mixture to a boil. Reduce the heat to low and simmer for 30 minutes. Serve with a dollop of yogurt or sour cream.

Serves 6.

Pea Soups

The pea—*Pisum sativum*, the "cultivated garden pea"—is indeed a venerable legume, with a long history of cultivation. Its fossilized remains have been found in Swiss lake villages that were inhabited as long as 6,000 years ago. No one knows just where the pea originated, however, though India seems likely, for the root of the word is Sanskrit. It was, along with wheat, probably one of the first edible plants that people domesticated when they abandoned their hunting-gathering ways in favor of staying put and exercising at least some control over their food supply. The first appearance of the word *pea* in English occurred around A.D. 725. Considerably later, Thomas Jefferson, a master gardener if ever there was one, grew 30 varieties and named peas his favorite vegetable, bar none. Peas are certainly good to eat any whichaway—fresh picked, frozen, dried, or raw. Straight out of the pod, they burst with sugar sweetness.

And you all know the nursery rhyme that comes from the turn of the century—18th into 19th: *Pease porridge hot, pease porridge cold, pease porridge in the pot nine days old. Some like it hot, some like it cold, some like it in the pot nine days old.*

We like ours hot and like to eat it right away.

Kick-Ass Pea Soup

Kick-Ass Pea Soup—that's what the elder of my sons has dubbed this family favorite. The reason is that it delivers a real wallop to hunger. It entered my repertoire when my son's city-bred, intellectually aristocratic father demanded what he called "peasant food"—steamy, down-to-earth, stick-to-your-ribs concoctions made of ingredients easily available to people living on the farms and in the rural villages of his native Germany. Our children were not great pea aficionados, but for some reason known only to the kitchen goddesses, not one of the four balked at this dish made of dried, split peas.

To make it, I've variously used green or yellow split peas. The choice depends on mood—spring leaves or sun. Toasted cheese sandwiches (we like Swiss or Edam) and applesauce are prime accompaniments.

Ingredients

1 pound split peas	¼ teaspoon garlic powder
2 quarts water	¼ teaspoon black pepper, freshly ground
1 meaty ham bone	¼ teaspoon dried marjoram
1 large onion, diced	1 teaspoon dried parsley
1 rib celery, diced	salt to taste
1 carrot, diced	

• Place the split peas, water, and ham bone in a large soup pot. Bring to a boil. Reduce heat and simmer for 1 hour. Remove the ham bone and cut off all the meat, discarding the bone but returning the meat to the pot.

• Add the onion, celery, carrot, garlic, pepper, marjoram, and parsley to the pot. Simmer for 1½ hours more. Add salt to taste and serve.

Serves at least 6. Freezes well.

Spicy Pea Soup

When I first met Melissa Walker, a lean and lithe resident of Decatur, Georgia, she looked boyishly elegant under a rakish Stetson. The event that brought us together was a gathering of southern nature writers on Ossabaw Island, one of the sea islands off the coast of Georgia. One occasion for the Stetson was Melissa's devotion to the West. In addition to editing *Reading the Environment*, a collection of pieces on the natural world, she's written *Down from the Mountaintop*, a close look at several novels written by black women in response to the civil rights movement. A second occasion for the hat was Melissa's baldness—she had just finished a grueling round of chemotherapy to combat cancer. That was four years ago. She's a winner. So is this soup.

She tells me that she and her husband, Jerome, concocted it about 10 years ago when he became, as she puts it, "a committed vegetarian." She says, "I who am perfectly happy eating chicken, fish, and the occasional hamburger was challenged with 'what to cook.' After finding that red and black beans did not agree with me, we decided to try the split pea. Jerome and I got in the kitchen one Saturday and played with peas, cilantro, and other spices. We came up with this soup. Even our finicky grandchildren like it."

Note: Make this one in a large stockpot, not a 5-quart soup pot. The recipe may be halved.

Ingredients

2 pounds green split peas

12 cups water

2–3 medium onions, chopped

6–8 cloves garlic, chopped

1 tablespoon olive oil (more, if desired)

8–10 small new or Yukon Gold potatoes, or 4 large potatoes, unpeeled and cubed

1 bunch fresh cilantro, or 2 tablespoons dried

2 heaping teaspoons cumin

1 heaping teaspoon ground coriander

1 teaspoon black pepper

salt to taste

- Wash the split peas. Place them in a large stockpot and cover with 2 inches of water. Bring to a boil, then reduce the heat and simmer for 30 minutes.

- Sauté the onions and garlic in the olive oil. Add to the peas, then add the potatoes. Stir in the cilantro, cumin, coriander, and pepper. Simmer for 45 minutes.

- Puree half of the soup in a blender. Mix it with the soup still in the pot. Simmer briefly and ladle into bowls.

Serves "two people for five or so meals," says Melissa.

Black-Eyed Pea Soup

Black-eyed peas, also known as cowpeas, crowder peas, and southern peas, aren't truly peas at all, though they're members of the same family. Formally, they're called *Vigna unguiculata*—"Vigna's clawed bean." The genus name honors Dominico Vigna, a professor of botany at the University of Pisa early in the 1600s. Why "clawed," I do not know, though I have grown these plants; the peas form in slender, foot-long pods without a sign of anything resembling a claw. The plant, an annual, is probably native to Africa and the Middle East but traveled early on to the Mediterranean and to China. Explorers and colonists brought it to the New World. In the American South today, it's cultivated as a forage crop for livestock as well as for its humanly edible peas. As an item traditionally eaten on New Year's Day to ensure good luck for the year to come, it has claimed a place of honor in the South.

Because my version of the soup uses mainly canned ingredients, it is one of the easiest and quickest to prepare—45 minutes at most from start to finish.

Ingredients

2 tablespoons olive oil

2 large onions, finely diced

4 large cloves garlic, pressed

2 14½-ounce cans chicken broth

2 15-ounce cans black-eyed peas, drained and rinsed

1 14½-ounce can diced tomatoes

1 8-ounce can tomato sauce

2 teaspoons dried oregano

¼ teaspoon red pepper flakes

1 bay leaf

pinch of cumin

juice of 1 lemon

salt and pepper to taste

- Place the oil in a large soup pot and heat over medium heat. Add the onions and garlic. Sauté until the onions are translucent, about 8 minutes.

- Add the chicken broth, black-eyed peas, tomatoes, tomato sauce, oregano, red pepper flakes, bay leaf, and cumin. Bring to a boil. Reduce the heat and simmer for 15 minutes.

- Stir in the lemon juice. Season to taste and ladle into bowls.

Serves 8.

Pigeon Pea Soup

Pigeon peas aren't "peas" any more than black-eyed peas are. They're so named because of their small size. They look like minuscule bird eggs, tiny light brown ovals swirled with fine red streaks. No one knows where this tropical vine, a member of the large legume family, originated—Africa, perhaps, or Southeast Asia. Its botanical name is *Cajanus cajan*, formed from the Malay word *cat-jana;* among its legion of common names are Congo pea, red gram, no-eye pea, the Hispanic *gandul*, India's *toovar dal*, China's *mu dou*, and the Swahili *mbassi*. Wherever it came from, it's been one of the world's important food crops from ancient times on. The Egyptians are known to have cultivated it before 2000 B.C. Nor are its edible "peas" the vine's only useful part: *C. cajan* serves as a cover crop; hedging; a training support for vanilla; material for basketry and thatching; and medicine. In the rural pharmacopoeia, pigeon peas are variously thought to stop bleeding, reduce a fever, heal wounds, and act as a diuretic and laxative. In India, pigeon peas are used as a remedy for colic; in Trinidad, they counteract witchcraft; and elsewhere, they're applied to bat bites or eaten to eliminate vertigo. Obviously, they're good for us in more ways than one.

And here's an easy way of converting these little legumes into a potent and delicious cure-all. The recipe is basic and may be prepared with almost any dried legume. But for their history and their faintly sweet flavor, use pigeon peas, which may be found in the Hispanic foods section of most supermarkets. The recipe can be gussied up, of course, with spices and herbs of your choosing.

Ingredients

1 pound dried pigeon peas

¼ pound salt pork, diced

6 cups chicken stock (see page 179)

1 large onion, diced

1 clove garlic, pressed

1 rib celery, chopped

1 large carrot, peeled and diced

1 bay leaf

salt and pepper to taste

- Soak the beans overnight and drain.

- Combine all the ingredients in a large soup pot. Bring to a boil. Reduce the heat, cover, and simmer for 2 to 3 hours, or until the peas are tender. Discard the bay leaf. Ladle into bowls.

Serves 6. Freezes well.

Lentil Soups

Lens culinaris, the "lens for cooking," was named for the shape of its seed. No one knows where lentils originated—it may have been southwestern Asia—but, like beans and peas, they were anciently cultivated. The flat little seeds have been found in Swiss lake villages dating back to the Bronze Age. Egypt and Greece certainly esteemed them and grew them abundantly in prebiblical times. And the Bible mentions them; in the King James version of Genesis, we read that the red pottage for which Esau traded his birthright to his younger twin, Jacob, was a "pottage of lentiles"—a lentil soup. (Lentils come in almost as many colors as Joseph's coat: red, white, green, orange, purple, and brown, the last being the kind we usually find on supermarket shelves.) Today, India is the largest producer, with significant crops also growing in the Middle East and North Africa. In the United States, lentils are grown mostly in Washington and Idaho. Wherever they come from, they're excellent sources of protein, vitamin B, iron, and phosphorus.

The best description of a meal centered on lentil soup comes from the novelist Laurence Sterne (1713–1768), who also wrote a travel memoir about a six-month journey through France and Italy. He tells a tale of arriving one day at the little farmhouse of a French peasant, where he takes note of the man and his large extended family "all sitting down together to their lentil-soup; a large wheaten loaf was in the middle of the table; and a flaggon of wine at each end promised joy through the stages of the repast—'twas a feast of love."

Oh, yes! I offer two recipes here for lentil soup love-feasts, one a mild brown pottage, the other a spicy red. The red version may also be made with brown lentils, and if you'd like to try some other colors, like green, they are available at reasonable prices over the Internet at, among other sites, epicurious.com and ethnicgrocer.com.

Linsensuppe

I've always called this one by its German name, for the Berlin-born father of my children first urged me to make it. Along with pea soup, he deemed it "peasant food," hearty, filling, and readily stirred up from ingredients available to German country folk. It's been a family favorite for decades. And my present husband, the Chief, gobbles it down right merrily.

Several variations may be worked on it:

- Put leftover beef or pork gravy (but not lamb or poultry) into the pot along with the lentils and stock.
- Replace 3 cups of stock with 3 cups of tomato juice.
- Add *Spätzle*—egg dumplings—for the last 20 minutes of cooking. The recipe is given on page 194.

Ingredients

1½ cups lentils

6 cups beef stock (see page 177)

1 medium onion, diced

2 small carrots, diced

2 ribs celery, diced

1½ cups canned tomatoes

1 tablespoon bacon grease

3 frankfurters, sliced thin

salt and pepper to taste

- Place the lentils and stock in a large soup pot. Cover and simmer for about 40 minutes.

- Add the onion, carrots, celery, tomatoes, and bacon grease. Simmer, covered, for 30 more minutes. Add the sliced frankfurters and simmer for yet another 30 minutes, adding more stock or water as necessary. Season to taste.

Serves 6. Freezes well—but better without the Spätzle, which may be added when the soup is cooking after being thawed.

Spicy Red Lentil Pottage

The ingredients of this soup meld into a lovely gold, flecked with shreds of orange carrot and red pepper flakes. The so-called red lentils are actually light orange, paler than carrot, before they're cooked; with simmering, they blanche to a straw color. To accompany the soup, I enjoy crackers with cheese, especially Fontina and an extra-sharp or horseradish cheddar, with a tangerine for sweetness.

The flavor is reminiscent of Indian cuisine. To make it more authentic, add:

- ½ teaspoon curry powder along with the other spices and lemon juice

Ingredients

¼ cup olive oil

2 onions, coarsely chopped

3 cloves garlic, pressed

4 cups chicken stock (see page 179)

6 cups water

2 cups red lentils

2 carrots, peeled and grated

2 ribs celery, finely diced

1 teaspoon sugar

1 dried red pepper, pressed, or ¼ teaspoon red pepper flakes

1 teaspoon ground coriander

1 teaspoon cumin

½ teaspoon paprika

2 teaspoons lemon zest

juice of two lemons

salt and pepper to taste

- Put the oil in a large soup pot and heat over medium low. Add the onions and garlic. Sauté over low heat, stirring constantly, until the onions are translucent, about 3 minutes.

- Pour the stock and water into the pot. Bring to a boil. Add the lentils, carrots, and celery. Cook at a low boil for 20 minutes. Reduce the heat to low.

- Add the sugar, red pepper, coriander, cumin, paprika, lemon zest, and lemon juice. Cover the pot and simmer for 45 minutes. Add water if necessary. Season with salt and pepper, and ladle into bowls.

Serves 8. Freezes well.

Chapter Three
Beefed-Up Soups and Other
Meaty Treats

As the offspring of a general farmer, who variously raised dairy cows, beef cattle, sheep, and the occasional pig—along with a prodigiously bountiful truck garden—my brothers, sisters, and I were served many a home-raised, home-grown soup. And here, with a few modern variations, are some of our down-home recipes.

Beef

The milk cows that my father raised were reddish gold Jerseys and Guernseys the color of caramel; the beef cattle, white-faced red Herefords, black Angus, and creamy white Charolais. Like all breeds that originated in Europe, they are collectively known as *Bos taurus*, with the genus designated by a Greek word and the species by one that is Latin. With emphatic redundancy, the formal name translates as "bull bull." And, oh, the cow has been ever important since it was first domesticated some 12 to 14 millennia ago. The Greek soldiers fighting at Troy sacrificed cattle to the gods, burned the carcasses, and feasted on the roasted meat till they could hold no more. Masai herdsmen in Kenya measure wealth in terms of cattle and rely greatly on the milk, blood, and meat of their animals for food. And if you believe the movies, the rise of the American West depended on cowboys and cattle drives. Whatever the era, wherever the place, beef and its gelatin-producing bones have figured as staple ingredients for soup.

Here, then, are four recipes, including one that offers a fine way to use the meat left after making beef stock; another that employs oxtails, a thrifty and old-fashioned cut; and one in which beef and vegetables commingle. The unleavened Australian bread known as damper (page 190) is a fit companion for any of these.

Beef with Barley Soup

Beef is the heart of this soup; barley, its essential substance; and sweet parsnips, its flavorful soul. I had forgotten how good parsnips are until I endeavored to re-create my mother's recipe. The recipe below is not exactly her version but rather the result of pinch-of-this, touch-of-that experiments. She did not use herbs and mushrooms, but they give pleasing flavor to the broth. Nor did she cook the onions and mushrooms, parsnips and carrots separately, but simmered them in the soup along with the beef and barley until they were tender. I prefer, however, to add the vegetables after they've been cooked on their own, a step that can be accomplished while the stock, barley, and herbs are melding. As for the meat, beef bites left from making stock are easier to use than beef stew meat, which must first be simmered in stock until it's tender and then cut into bite-sized pieces.

Variation: This recipe also works wonders when made with pork stock and meat reserved from making the stock.

Ingredients

8 cups beef stock (see page 177)

½ cup pearl barley

½ teaspoon dried thyme

½ teaspoon dried marjoram

½ teaspoon dried oregano

1 tablespoon butter

1 large onion, diced

4 cloves garlic, finely diced

½ pound fresh mushrooms, cut into small chunks

1 medium parsnip, diced

1 medium carrot, diced

2 cups beef bites saved from making stock, or 1 pound beef stew

    meat cut into bite-sized pieces and simmered in stock until tender

salt and pepper to taste

•   Put the stock, barley, thyme, marjoram, and oregano in a large soup pot and bring to a boil. Reduce the heat and simmer, covered, for 1 hour.

•   Meanwhile, melt the butter in a small skillet over medium-low heat. Add the onion and garlic and sauté, stirring frequently, for 10 minutes, or until soft and translucent. Add mushrooms and sauté, stirring frequently, until they are cooked, about 10 minutes. Then add the onion, garlic, and mushroom mixture to the barley broth.

•   As the onions, garlic, and mushrooms are cooking, bring a saucepan of water to a boil. Add the parsnips and carrots and boil them until they are tender, about 4 minutes. Drain.

•   Stir the beef bites, parsnips, and carrots into the soup. Simmer for 15 minutes. Season to taste and ladle into bowls.

Serves 6. Freezes well.

Minnie's Meat Soup

This one revels in an outlandishly original use for the meat with which it's cooked. The recipe comes from Donna Lewis, who also contributed Harvest Minestrone (page 43) and Tunisian Vegetable Stew (page 44). And it's an heirloom, inherited from a much-loved honorary aunt, who was born in Brooklyn, New York, not long after the dawn of the 20th century. Minnie's heritage was Sicilian, and she learned to cook from her mother and other relatives, who all lived together on various floors of a brick house in an Italian neighborhood. The extended family raised tomatoes in the yard, hauled them upstairs at harvest, and dried them on the fire escape. They canned much tomato paste and made their own spaghetti, which was dried in strips laid over the beds. As for Minnie herself, Donna describes her this way: "She was a fun-loving, petite woman but with the heart and temper of a lioness. Any Italian dishes I make were given to me by her instruction and observation. I then had to face the critique, which was sometimes brutal." She gave Donna several now-treasured handwritten recipes, of which this is one (except that I've added measurements). Minnie's own comments on her meat soup are enclosed below in quotation marks.

This is a 2-day soup. On the first day, the fragrance of the stock as it simmers down is glorious and due to the secret ingredient, the cinnamon stick. On the second day, the odd thing is that the meat, which was part of the stock, is not returned to the soup. Instead, it later becomes the focal point of a special salad that accompanies the soup. For salad greens, Minnie used escarole, but that's not always easy to find. So I have combined romaine, bibb lettuce, and spinach to make the bed for the meat and onion. But her instructions for an oregano vinaigrette are given below. Serve salad and soup with a large loaf of crusty bread.

Day 1: The Stock

Ingredients

2 tablespoons olive oil

1½ pounds lean beef (London broil, rump roast), sliced into 1-inch strips

1½ pounds marrowbones

1 large onion, unpeeled, quartered

1 carrot, unpeeled, sliced in half crosswise

1 bunch flat-leaved Italian parsley

1 bay leaf

1 stick cinnamon

12 peppercorns

14 cups water

• Heat the oil in a large heavy skillet. Lightly brown the beef on all sides, about 3 minutes each.

• Place the beef and marrowbones in a large soup pot. Add the onion, carrot, parsley, bay leaf, cinnamon, peppercorns, and water. Bring to a boil. Reduce the heat and simmer until about half the water has evaporated, about 6 to 7 hours.

• "After the meat is cooked, you will have a nice broth." Strain it through cheesecloth. Reserve the meat but discard everything else ("You don't want any large chunks in the broth"). Refrigerate the stock overnight so that the fat will congeal and be easily removed.

Makes about 8 cups.

Day 2: The Soup and Salad

Ingredients

8 cups beef stock

1 cup orzo

salt and pepper to taste

Romano cheese, freshly grated

salad greens

beef from the stock, cut into bite-sized pieces

red onion slices

"a tasty dressing of olive oil, vinegar, oregano, salt, and pepper"

- Soup as the first course: Put the stock into a large soup pot. Bring to a boil. Add the orzo and boil gently for 6 minutes, or until the orzo is al dente. Season to taste, ladle into bowls, and garnish with cheese.

- Salad as the second course: "Now the salad: Cut the meat into pieces. Tear the greens up on salad plates, place the cut-up meat on the greens, and top with thinly sliced red onions." Add oregano vinaigrette and serve, along with butter and a great loaf of crusty bread—the kind that you tear into small chunks.

Serves 4. The soup freezes well.

Oxtail Soup

Making soup from oxtails was once a thrifty practice: None of the ox (bull, steer, or cow, as the case may be) was wasted, including the circular tailbones, surrounded by meat and fat. Today, you can't expect to find oxtails stocked at many meat counters. But you can ask for them, as I have done at my favorite supermarket. When they arrive, the meat manager calls, and off I zoom to put in a good supply.

Oxtail soup is also one of those virtuous soups that make their own stock. As a result, it's a 2-day soup—almost all day on the first day for preparing the stock, an hour at most on the second for stirring up the soup. Or the stock can be frozen, along with the meat, until you're good and ready for the soup.

Day I: The Stock

Ingredients

4 pounds oxtails

14 cups water

- The first step is roasting the oxtails. Preheat the oven to 500˚ Fahrenheit. Place the oxtails in a shallow roasting pan. Roast for 15 minutes, then turn the tails over and roast for another 15 minutes. Remove the oxtails from the pan and place them in a stockpot.

- Pour off the fat from the roasting pan. Place the pan on the stove and pour in 1 cup water. Bring to a boil and scrape off browned bits of meat. Pour the liquid over the oxtails in the stockpot.

- Pour 10 cups water over the bones. Bring to a boil. Reduce the heat and simmer for 3 hours, skimming off foam as necessary.

- Remove the oxtails. When they have cooled, remove the meat and reserve it. Put the bones back into the pot. Add the remaining water. Bring to a boil, reduce the heat, and simmer for 5 to 6 hours. Add more water as necessary to keep the bones covered.

- Strain through cheesecloth, discarding the bones. Cool to room temperature, then refrigerate overnight.

- Remove the fat from the top of the stock. Use right away or freeze.

Day 2: The Soup

Ingredients

3 tablespoons corn oil

1 large onion, chopped

2 medium leeks (white and pale green parts only), chopped

2 medium parsnips, peeled and diced

2 carrots, peeled and shredded

4 cloves garlic, minced

1 teaspoon dried thyme

1 bay leaf

7 cups oxtail stock, or 3 14½-ounce cans beef broth

½ cup dry sherry

2 cups oxtail meat

2 large potatoes, peeled and cut into ½-inch cubes

- Heat the oil in a large soup pot. Add the onion, leeks, parsnips, carrots, garlic, thyme, and bay leaf, and sauté over medium heat until the onion is translucent, about 10 minutes.

- Add the stock, sherry, and meat. Bring to a boil and add the potatoes. Reduce the heat and simmer, covered, for 20 minutes, or until the potatoes are tender. Ladle into bowls.

Serves 6. Does not freeze well because of the potatoes.

Beef Soup with Vegetables

Here, beef and vegetables come together joyfully. And they make for a hearty meal-in-one—protein, carbohydrates, vitamins galore. I like to top off a supper centered on this soup with muffins and fresh pears. My muffin recipe is found on page 191.

Ingredients

2 pounds tender beef (like sirloin or round steak), cut into ½-inch cubes

8 cups beef stock (see page 177)

2 8-ounce cans tomato sauce

1 14½-ounce can diced tomatoes

1 large onion, diced

3 ribs celery, diced

3 carrots, peeled and diced

6 cloves garlic, pressed

2 medium potatoes, peeled and cut into ½-inch cubes

2 bay leaves

4 ounces button mushrooms, cut into small chunks

1 15-ounce can dark red kidney beans, undrained

1 15-ounce can cannellini beans, undrained

salt and pepper to taste

- Combine all the ingredients except the beans, salt, and pepper in a heavy soup pot. Bring to a boil. Reduce the heat, cover, and simmer for 1 hour, stirring occasionally.

- Add the beans with their juices to the soup. Cover and keep simmering until the meat is tender, about 30 minutes. Season to taste and ladle into bowls.

Serves 6. Freezes well.

Lamb

Useful for meat, milk, and fleece, sheep have been domesticated for at least 7,000 years. The animal's formal moniker, *Ovis aries*, comes from Latin and means (in the often reduplicate fashion of those who name the earth's creatures) "sheep ram." My father raised them, along with his cows and hogs. Turned loose on our 4-acre front yard, they served as lawn mowers as well as suppliers of wool and dinner. But from chops and roasts to stew and soup, the lamb that I ate as a child was usually mutton, which came not from a young animal but from a fully mature sheep, a creature much suited, like a tough, old chicken, to long simmering with vegetables and seasonings. These days we have access to tender cuts of meat year-round, thanks to modern marketing and transportation. Nonetheless, a leg of lamb can seem as eternal as a ham or turkey. Here's a good way to relish it to the very last slurp.

Scotch Broth

This soup is redolent of tradition, of shepherds herding their flocks on windy moors. Its name harks back to 1834, but this country soup is surely older than that. And it's a 2-day soup, one for making stock from meaty bones, the second for simmering with vegetables. Barley is also a time-honored ingredient, but potatoes may be used instead, and if you'd like a soup with more body, leftover mashed potatoes act as a fine thickener.

This soup, like oxtail, has the virtue of making its own stock as it cooks.

Day I: The Stock

Ingredients

2 pounds lamb shanks or meaty lamb bones

water to cover by 2 inches

• Place the lamb shanks or meaty bones in a large stockpot. Cover with water. Bring to a boil. Reduce the heat and simmer for 6 hours.

• Remove the meat and bones, discarding bones and fell, if any. When it's cool, cut the meat into bite-sized pieces and refrigerate.

• Cool the stock to room temperature and refrigerate.

Day II: The Soup

Ingredients

10 cups lamb stock

1 10-ounce package pearl onions, blanched for 1 minute, cooled in cold water, and peeled

3 carrots, peeled and cut into ¼-inch rounds

1 turnip, peeled and diced

2 cloves garlic, minced

1 bay leaf

½ cup pearl barley or 1 large potato, peeled and cubed

1½ tablespoons butter

4 ounces fresh mushrooms, cut into small chunks

• Place the stock, onions, carrots, turnip, garlic, and bay leaf into a large soup pot. Bring to a boil. Reduce the heat and simmer for 1 hour.

• Add the barley and simmer for 45 minutes.

• Meanwhile, heat the butter in a skillet over medium heat. Add the mushrooms and sauté for 10 minutes, stirring frequently. Put the mushrooms in the soup and simmer for 15 minutes.

Serves 6 to 8. Freezes well.

Ham

Ham, bacon, pork chops, spareribs, chittlings—the domestic pig has been a source of food since pre-historic times. Its formal name is *Sus scrofa*, a pair of Latin words that translate somewhat redundantly into "pig sow." The animal that we know today originated from wild stock that roamed—still roams—the forests of Europe, Asia, and northern Africa. The New World, however, was totally pigless until Europeans introduced the creature in the earliest days of exploration. It's believed that they accompanied Christopher Columbus on his second voyage, which took place in 1493. Columbus or someone else—I remain eternally grateful.

As for ham, the word was used early on by the Anglo-Saxons, who surely appreciated the flavor and food value of a pig's plump, meaty thighs. My father certainly did, for he raised hogs and cured hams in the Virginia fashion, curing them with salt, spicing them with black pepper, cold-smoking them, then hanging them in the attic for a year. (It was an attic to which you ascended by stairs pulled down from the ceiling.) Virginia ham, however, is a mite salty for the soup pot, unless it is soaked first (apple juice is a good medium) or used sparingly. A suspicion of Virginia ham enlivens gumbos and bean soups.

Of the two soups offered here, the first represents an excellent way of using up the last meaty morsels of a ham that seems never ending. The second is lightning quick to put together, taking 20 minutes at most from cold start to steaming finish.

Ham, Vegetable, and Barley Soup

A meaty ham bone is ideal for this one. It furnishes not only stock but also meat for the soup proper. Make the stock according to the directions on page 180. Then cook the soup the following day. Or if you wish, use diced leftover ham and stock already made.

Note: Make this one in a large stockpot, not a 5-quart soup pot.

Ingredients

8 cups ham stock

3 cups cooked ham, cut into bite-sized cubes

2 medium potatoes, peeled and cut into ½-inch cubes

2 carrots, peeled and cut into ¼-inch rounds

1 parsnip, peeled, sliced lengthwise, and cut into 1/2-inch rounds

2 ribs celery, coarsely chopped

1 large onion, chopped

1 clove garlic, chopped

1 14½-ounce can diced tomatoes in juice

½ cup pearl barley

salt and pepper to taste

freshly grated Parmesan cheese (optional)

• Place all the ingredients except the cheese in a large soup pot. Bring to a boil. Reduce the heat and simmer over low heat for 40 minutes. Ladle into bowls and garnish with Parmesan cheese.

Serves 8. May be frozen but with some loss of quality, because potatoes do not like arctic temperatures.

Cow Puncher's Gullion

Gullion—what's *that?* Mary Faville, friend for 50 years and trainer of black Labradors that are often top dogs nationally in field trials, does not know, nor can she explain the *cow puncher* part of the name. She learned the recipe and its odd moniker from her mother. Once upon a time, in the days just before and after World War II, Mary and her family summered on a tiny island in Canada's Georgian Bay. The place abounded in pines and fish but lacked refrigeration and plumbing. The food

that they toted with them either came in cans or could last, like peanut butter and jelly, without an icebox. All of this belly-filling soup, except for the dry-stored garlic, belongs to the first category. Mary still summers on the island, but since the end of the 1940s, the cabin has housed a refrigerator that runs on propane gas.

As for the soup's peculiar name, I indulge in speculation. *Cow puncher* reminds me of an old-time chuck wagon, no more possessed of a refrigerator than the island. *Gullion*, I suspect, is an abbreviation of the word *slumgullion*, a bit of American slang used by Mark Twain, for one, back in 1872. An 1874 dictionary of slang defines it as "any cheap, nasty, washy beverage." I think that the name settled upon in the most human fashion—someone just plain liked the offbeat, highly original *sound* of the word.

The soup needs no extra salt. The ham and sauerkraut supply quite enough.

Ingredients

1 24-ounce canned ham, diced

    juice from the ham

1 15-ounce can pinto beans, undrained

1 15-ounce can dark red kidney beans, undrained

2 large cloves garlic, finely minced

1 28-ounce can tomatoes in juice

½–1 14-ounce can sauerkraut, drained and washed

1–2 cups water, depending on your preference for thick or somewhat thinner

•   Put all the ingredients into a large soup pot. Stir and cook over medium heat until everything is well heated. Ladle into bowls.

Serves 6 heartily. Freezes well.

Sausage

Sausage—the name originates in the Latin word *salsus*, which means "salted." Salt has long been a medium for drying and preserving meat. And sausage comes in as many guises as legumes or nationalities or appetites. Pork, beef, poultry—all may end up minced, seasoned, and stuffed into casings or offered as ground meat. The seasonings can range from mild to incendiary, with enough garlic to scare off witches. And many countries seem to have distinct sausage identities of their own—the German wursts, for example, and Polish kielbasa, French andouille, Spanish chorizo, Portuguese *linguiça*. The list is long enough to circle the world. One of our favorites is a bulk sausage produced by Tom's Sausage Company just north of the town of Stantonsburg in North Carolina—lustily hot and full of thyme. Crumbled and browned, it adds the perfecting touch to the Sausage and Bean Chowder just below.

Other soups in this cookbook use sausage, but Sausage and Bean Chowder relies on sausage for its basic flavor. So does its companion in this section, the well-spiced and meaty Portuguese Sausage Soup with Kale.

Sausage and Bean Chowder

The day of the outdoor oyster roast was blustery, the sky gray, and the air downright arctic. But that's not unusual for winter on the North Carolina coast. All the people in our yard were bundled up, of course, and we did have a cheerful wood fire in the Chief's outdoor hearth. The oysters sizzled and steamed. Nonetheless, if you stood still for any length of time, the cold stole into your very marrow. But Joyce Wixon, a neighbor, had a remedy—this soup, which effects a speedy thaw.

Ingredients

1 pound bulk sausage, hot or mild

1 14½-ounce can kidney beans

1 14½-ounce can tomatoes, chopped

1 large onion, diced

½ cup peeled and cubed potatoes

½ cup chopped green pepper

3/4 teaspoon salt

¼ teaspoon garlic powder

¼ teaspoon dried thyme

⅛ teaspoon black pepper

1 bay leaf

1 cup water or tomato juice

- Cook the sausage until brown. Pour off the fat. Reserve the meat.

- Combine the kidney beans, tomatoes, onion, potatoes, green pepper, salt, garlic powder, thyme, pepper, bay leaf, and water (or tomato juice) in a large soup pot. Add the sausage. Bring to a boil. Reduce the heat, cover, and simmer for 1 to 2 hours.

Serves 4. Freezes poorly.

Portuguese Sausage Soup with Kale

Shay Edwards, my college roommate half a century ago, introduced me to this full-bodied heirloom soup. Shay, living on Cape Cod and retired now from research work at the Woods Hole Marine Biology Laboratory, may often be found wielding a hammer on behalf of Habitat for Humanity.

Of the soup, she writes, "This recipe came from a Portuguese friend who got it from her mother, who got it from her mother, who got it from her mother. It's a wonderfully warming fall or winter meal when served with hunks of crusty bread. The ingredients make a whopping big pot of soup. I never cut the recipe and can usually refrigerate five to seven jars for lunches or emergency company."

She also suggests cooking it with a "Portuguese simmer," defined by Howard Mitcham in his *Provincetown Seafood Cookbook* as a simmer that "does not even boil or bubble; it's probably the world's slowest cooking, but it gets spectacular results." If you're curious about the sausages called for in the recipe, *linguiça* is Portuguese, while *chouriço* is the Portuguese word for the meat that Spanish-speaking people call chorizo. Both have a middling heat factor.

Kale adds a great green flavor to the spicy meats. Like cabbage, cauliflower, broccoli, and brussels sprouts, it belongs to the cabbage family and, also like them, bears the same botanical name, *Brassica oleracea*, "garden cabbage." Its group name distinguishes it from the others: Acephala, or "garden cabbage that does not form a head."

Shay offers a quick alternative to the cooking method given below: "I use cans of white pea beans or navy beans drained of liquid. I put all the ingredients into the pot at once, bring it to a simmer, put a lid on it, and let it do its thing for 4 or 5 hours—works just as well."

She's right; I've made it both ways. Either one produces an exceptionally tasty meal.

Note: This one must be made in a large stockpot, which will be full to brimming over before the kale cooks down.

Ingredients

1 pound dried small white beans (pea, navy, your choice)

1 marrowbone, sawed into chunks so that the marrow will seep out

4 country-style spareribs

water to cover

1 pound kale, washed, torn from stems, and chopped

1 pound *linguiça* sausage, casing removed and cut into ¼-inch rounds

1 pound *chouriço* sausage, casing removed and cut into ¼-inch rounds

1 pound cooked ham, cubed

4 medium potatoes, diced

2 small onions, sliced

6 cloves garlic, unpeeled

dash of crushed red pepper

salt (optional)

black pepper to taste

splash of cider vinegar

- Soak the beans overnight. Drain.

- Put the beans, marrowbones, and spareribs into a stockpot capable of holding at least 9 quarts. Cover with water and bring to a boil. Reduce the heat and boil gently for 1 hour.

- Add the kale, *linguiça, chouriço*, and ham. Bring to a boil. Reduce the heat and give the ingredients a Portuguese simmer for 1 hour.

- Add the potatoes, onions, garlic, red pepper, salt, black pepper, and vinegar. Simmer, uncovered for 5 or 6 hours. Add water as necessary to keep the ingredients covered. Remove and discard the bones. Ladle into bowls.

"Makes enough for 20 people or for 2 people with lots left over." Freezes well.

Chapter Four
A Bird in the Pot

bird in the pot is worth two in the bush. And what a grand array of birds there are to choose from—chickens and turkeys, of course; domestic or wild ducks and geese; guinea fowl; and even partridge, quail, grouse, and ring-necked pheasant. In the colonial years and the first years of the new United States, the variety of birds eaten was far greater than it is today. One early explorer of the Carolinas, John Lawson, listed the birds that he saw as he traveled—not only listed them but noted whether they were good to eat as well. Two-thirds of the species won his gustatory approval, including snipe, woodcock, and cedar waxwings. But pelicans and cormorants, in his opinion, were to be eaten only in case of dire emergency.

In this chapter, I concentrate on chickens and turkeys, with tips on making soup from ducks and geese. One pheasant recipe is also included for its sheer elegance.

Chicken

Once upon a time in India, some four millennia ago, a wild red jungle fowl, *Gallus gallus* (which translates as "cock cock"), became domesticated. But the reason for its taming had little to do with food, though the bird must have been served up more than occasionally for dinner. The primary interest of its keepers was in cockfighting, a bloody sport that spread rapidly throughout Asia and the Near East and arrived in Greece around the turn of the fifth century B.C. Not long thereafter, it made its way to Rome and thence into western Europe. Spanish conquistadores introduced the battling bird into the New World. Today, though the sport is widely outlawed, gamecocks still exist, gaudy, loudmouthed, and spurred with stiletto-like spikes. The breed is probably the closest living relative of that wild red ancestor, which is believed to be the progenitor of all modern chickens, be they bantams, Rhode Island reds, or exotics gussied up with crests and silky feathers.

It was only in the late 1800s that attention became focused on chicken as a prime source of both meat and eggs. Of course, the birds had run around in villages and barnyards since people had first noticed them and brought them home. But only young—and therefore tender—specimens were likely to be roasted, fried, or fricaseed. Old, tough chickens ended up in the stockpot. In her cookbook *The Virginia Housewife*, published in 1824, Mary Randolph gives a recipe for "Soup of Any Kind of Old Fowl," and describes it as "the only way in which they are eatable." The old fowl is cooped and fed moderately for 2 weeks, then killed and plucked. When the parts are separated, she advises throwing away the whole back, the skin, and the fat, "which are too gross and strong for use." The remaining pieces are stewed for 3½ hours, along with a pound of bacon, a large chopped onion, pepper and salt, mace, a handful of parsley, and 2 quarts of water. The soup is then thickened with "a large spoonful of butter rubbed into two of flour, the yelks [sic] of two eggs, and half a pint of milk."

Unless we raise them ourselves, we don't have old fowl these days. And many recipes for chicken soup call for boneless, skinless pieces cut from young, tender birds. But using such pieces, we lose the gelatin—and thus the protein—found in the bones. The way of getting around the strictures of recipes calling for no skin or bones is to make the stock from wings, thighs, or whole birds from which the skin and fat have been removed (see page 179) and to reserve the meat to put into the soup.

Chicken and Rice

This standard soup may be cooked up in two different ways, one using chicken stock, the other making its own stock as it simmers. The first method is just right for using the meat that's left after stock has been prepared—and it's quick, taking only 45 minutes. The second has been adapted from a recipe in *Bon Appétit*, which called for too much rice. It is a bit more time consuming, but equally delicious.

Chicken is the first magical ingredient here. Rice is the second. The formal name of this annual grass is *Oryza sativa*, which translates simply as "cultivated rice." And it has been cultivated for more than 5,000 years, with domestication taking place in India. Today, about half the population of the world depends upon this grain as a staple food.

> **Tip:** Instead of water and melted butter, use 2 cups of this soup to moisten an 8-ounce bag of commercial stuffing.

Method I

Ingredients

8 cups chicken stock, or 4 cups stock and 4 cups water (see page 179)

1 carrot, peeled and grated

1 rib celery, coarsely diced

1 onion, chopped

2 cloves garlic, chopped

2 teaspoons salt

1 bay leaf

½ cup rice

2 cups cooked chicken, cut into bite-sized pieces

freshly grated Parmesan cheese (optional)

- Place 7 cups of the chicken stock in a large soup pot. Add the carrot, celery, onion, garlic, salt, and bay leaf. Bring to a boil. Reduce the heat and simmer, covered, for 30 minutes.

- As the stock, veggies, and seasonings are simmering, bring the remaining cup of stock to a boil. Add the rice, reduce the heat to low, and simmer for about 15 minutes, until the rice is tender.

- Add the chicken pieces to the soup pot. Stir in the rice. Let this simmer, uncovered, until warmed thoroughly. Garnish, if you'd like, with freshly grated Parmesan.

Serves 6. Freezes well.

Method II

Ingredients

8 cups water

2 chicken breasts, skin and fat removed

4 chicken thighs, skin and fat removed

1 carrot, peeled and halved lengthwise

1 onion, coarsely chopped

1 rib celery, quartered

2 cloves garlic, chopped

2 teaspoons salt

1 bay leaf

½ cup uncooked long-grain white rice

salt and pepper to taste

freshly grated Parmesan cheese

• Combine the water, chicken, carrot, onion, celery, garlic, salt, and bay leaf in a large soup pot. Bring to a boil. Reduce the heat, cover, and simmer until the chicken is cooked, about 35 minutes. With a slotted spoon, transfer the chicken and carrot to a platter. Let cool slightly, and pull the chicken meat off bones in bite-sized pieces; set aside. Discard the bones. Slice the carrot into $\frac{1}{4}$-inch pieces, and reserve.

• Strain the broth through cheesecloth or a fine sieve. Discard the solids. Pour 1 cup of the broth into a medium saucepan. Bring to a boil. Add the rice, and return to a boil. Reduce the heat to low; cover and cook until the broth is absorbed and the rice is tender, about 15 minutes.

• Return the remaining broth, chicken pieces, and sliced carrot to the large soup pot. Stir in the cooked rice. Season with salt and pepper. Just before serving, garnish with Parmesan.

Serves 6. Freezes well.

Chicken Noodle Picante

This one zings. Ginger and hot peppers inspire it with a subtle bite, which can be heightened or diminished according to the numbers of peppers used and whether they are fresh or dried. It may be obvious by now that I'm enamored of cayenne peppers, which we grow every summer in hot red abundance. Botanically, they are *Capsicum annuum*, "annual plant with a bite." Their heat factor is equal to that of Tabasco and greater by far than that of jalapeño. Peppers, native to Central and South America, were domesticated long before the arrival of the conquistadores, who came, saw, ingested, and gave them to the rest of the world. As for ginger, it is native to the Far East, perhaps Malaysia and southern China. The first part of its scientific name, *Zingiber officinale* or "ginger used for food and medicine," traces back to that part of the world. And it has been domesticated for so long that it has lost one of the attributes of most plants—its seeds. For millennia, ginger has been propagated only by splitting its roots and replanting them.

For this recipe, bone-in chicken, skinned and defatted, may be used in place of the breasts called for. Start by putting the meat into a large stockpot and covering with at least 2 inches of water. When the pieces are cooked through, remove the bones and return the meat to the pot, along with the other ingredients mentioned in the first step.

Ingredients

6 cups chicken stock (see page 179)

3 cups water

1 large onion, diced

6 cloves garlic, finely chopped

1 1-inch piece of ginger, unpeeled and cut into 2 or 3 chunks

3 whole dried hot red peppers (preferably cayenne), or 1 crumbled

8 ounces boneless, skinless chicken breasts, cut into bite-sized pieces

6 ounces angel-hair pasta

4 scallions, finely chopped

•   Combine the stock, water, onion, garlic, ginger, and peppers in a large stockpot. Bring to a boil over high heat. Reduce the heat to low and simmer for 5 minutes. Add the chicken and cook for 5 minutes, or until the meat is no longer pink in the center. Test by cutting a piece in half.

•   Add the pasta. Cook, stirring with a fork, for 2 minutes or until the pasta is tender. Remove the ginger and peppers (unless you've used a crumbled pepper). Ladle the soup into bowls and sprinkle with scallions.

Serves 6. Freezes well.

Chicken and Pasta Soup

Coriander, cilantro, cumin, fennel, and lemon zest, plus lemon juice, mingle intimately in this soup to give it distinctive flavor. The chicken and pasta furnish it with a truly tummy-filling body. Many kinds of small-sized pasta can be used; I favor little shells, ditalini, or orecchiette (which means "little ear"). As for fresh cilantro, it's carried by many supermarkets in the produce section. To save a run to the store when it's needed, though, I usually keep at least a cup of the chopped herb in the freezer. But because cilantro doesn't make everybody happy, its use here is optional.

Cilantro and coriander are intimately conjoined twins. Their flavors are decidedly different, with coriander tasting like citrus, and cilantro, sometimes called green coriander, claiming a pungent aroma and a somewhat soapy taste, but they are actually two incarnations of the same plant—fruit and leaves, respectively. Native to Greece and the eastern Mediterranean, the plant was anciently prized. Coriander was one of the foodstuffs entombed with Egypt's Tutankhamen, who died in 1352 B.C. Coriander followed the Silk Road to China in the sixth century A.D. and came to the Americas with the Spanish conquistadores. When I make this soup, its fragrance brings thoughts of a line of cooks at least two millennia long.

Variation: Make this soup with potato dumplings (page 195) instead of pasta.

Ingredients

1 tablespoon olive oil

2 skinless, boneless chicken breasts (about 12 ounces)

salt and pepper

2 large onions, coarsely chopped

3 plum tomatoes, peeled and sliced

1 tablespoon lemon zest

2 tablespoons coriander seeds

2 tablespoons cumin seeds

2 tablespoons fennel seeds

8 cups chicken stock (see page 179) or canned broth

½ cup chopped, fresh cilantro (optional)

1 cup small pasta shells, ditalini, or orecchiette, freshly cooked

3 plum tomatoes, seeded and chopped

juice of 2 fresh lemons (about ½ cup)

• Heat the oil in a large soup pot over medium-high heat. Sprinkle the chicken with salt and pepper and sauté until cooked through, about 4 minutes for each side. Transfer the chicken to a plate and let cool.

• Add the onions, sliced tomatoes, coriander, cumin, fennel, and lemon zest to the pot and sauté over medium heat until aromatic, about 2 minutes. Add the stock and ¼ cup of the cilantro. Simmer for 20 minutes.

• Strain the broth into a large heavy-duty pot. Cut the cooked chicken into bite-sized pieces and add to the broth.

• Add the cooked pasta (which can be prepared while broth is simmering). Add the chopped tomatoes, lemon juice, and remaining ¼ cup cilantro. Bring the soup to a simmer to heat the ingredients through and through. Ladle into bowls.

Serves 6. Freezes well—except when the soup contains potato dumplings.

Chicken Gumbo

Okra is synonymous with gumbo. Science has dubbed the plant with its slender green pods *Abelmoschus esculentus*, "edible musk" for its musk-scented seeds. It's the one and only edible member of the large mallow family, which includes hollyhocks and cotton. Though it's native to Asia, the names by which we know it came out of Africa, a heritage from the days of the slave trade, when it became widely cultivated in the West Indies. In the early 19th century, its pods sported thorns around the base, and the pods themselves were ribby, narrow, and pointed, but these characteristics have long been bred out of the plant. The word *okra* is West African, and *gumbo*, referring to the same plant, is Bantu in origin. The latter has slid over to denominate a thickened soup made of vegetables, rice, and various meats, like chicken, hot sausage, or shrimp. The thickening is due to okra: The pods are full of a jellylike substance that adds considerable body to the liquid they're cooked in.

Recipes for gumbos exist by the thousands. I like this one because of its simplicity—the ease of making the flour-and-oil roux (*roux* is a lovely French word that means "browned"), the use of frozen okra, the short hour and a half from start to slurp. The okra, not incidentally, does not require thawing before you cut it into chunks. And here are other ingredients that you might enjoy:

- a handful of country ham, cut into small chunks, to be tossed at the same time as the chicken
- a healthy spoonful of cooked long-grain rice in the center of each serving

Ingredients

¼ cup vegetable oil

¼ cup flour

1 onion, diced

2 cloves garlic, pressed

1 dried cayenne pepper, crumbled, or 1 teaspoon ground cayenne

1 10-ounce package frozen whole okra, cut into chunks

1 red bell pepper, seeded and chopped

4 cups chicken stock (see page 179)

2 14½-ounce cans diced tomatoes

1 bay leaf

1 teaspoon dried thyme

1 pound boneless, skinless chicken breast tenders, cut into 1-inch pieces

salt and pepper to taste

• Place the oil and flour in the bottom of a large soup pot. Cook over medium-high heat, stirring constantly, until the roux begins to acquire a warm brown color, about 5 minutes.

• Mix the onions, garlic, and cayenne pepper into the roux. Turn off the heat. Stir frequently until the onions are soft and the pot no longer sizzles.

• Return the pot to medium heat. Stir in the okra and bell pepper. Cook for 5 minutes, stirring frequently. Add the chicken stock, tomatoes, bay leaf, and thyme. Let simmer for 5 more minutes.

• Add the chicken to the soup. Bring to a boil. Reduce the heat and simmer, uncovered, for 30 minutes. Sprinkle in salt and pepper to taste. Ladle into bowls.

Serves 6. Freezes well.

South-of-the-Border Chicken Soup

Chili powder and cilantro flavor this version of a classic soup that contains not-so-subtle hints of Mexico. And it has another virtue apart from its taste: No more than half an hour is needed to prepare it.

As with any classic, it comes in a host of variations. Here are two suggested by my Arabic-speaking cousin, Betty Hayford, who lives in Evanston, Illinois, with her Chinese-speaking husband. Of her version, she says, "The addition of lime shells makes for a nice, piquant mix of flavors." Indeed, it does:

- For a real jolt of lime, put not only the juice in the soup but also the lime rinds.
- For a truly Mexican touch, leave out the cooked rice. Instead, use 4 corn tortillas. As the soup is simmering, halve the tortillas, cut them into strips, and cook them in 3 tablespoons hot oil until they are crisp. Pat the strips with paper towels to remove excess oil, and keep them warm in a low oven.

Ingredients

2 tablespoons olive oil

1 pound chicken breast tenders, cut into bite-sized cubes

1 medium onion, coarsely chopped

1 large red bell pepper, coarsely chopped

1 large clove garlic, pressed

1 jalapeño pepper, seeded and minced

2 teaspoons chili powder

4 cups chicken stock (see page 179)

1 10-ounce package frozen corn kernels

1 cup cooked long-grain white rice

1 teaspoon chopped fresh cilantro or parsley

juice of 1 lime

salt and pepper to taste

• Heat the oil over medium heat in a large soup pot. Add the chicken, onion, bell pepper, garlic, jalapeño, and chili powder. Cook for 5 minutes, stirring frequently.

• Add the stock, corn, and rice. Bring to a boil. Reduce the heat and simmer for 6 minutes, or until the chicken is tender. Stir in the cilantro and lime juice. Season to taste and ladle into bowls.

Serves 4. Freezes well.

Cock-a-Leekie Soup

The first literary reference in English to cock-a-leekie soup comes from 1771, in a play, *Maid of Bath*, by Samuel Foote. One character says, "The bride's dinner shall be furnished by me." A second character responds, "Cock-a-leekie soup." We can be sure, however, that the soup predates 1771 by a long shot. It was surely an ideal way of stewing an old, tough fowl into pure deliciousness. But to my astonishment, neither of my two editions of that classic cookbook *The Joy of Cooking* suggests returning the meat to the pot once the stock is made.

Along with the chicken, leeks impart a primary flavor to this soup. They are kissing cousins to onions, garlic, and chives, and anyone who fancies the genus *Allium* will rejoice in cock-a-leekie soup. We may thank the Romans for bringing *A. porrum*, "garlic leek," a native of the eastern Mediterranean and the Middle East, to Europe and Britain. The number of leeks used depends on their size, for they grow in diameters that range from modest to humongous.

Ingredients

1 whole chicken (3–3½ pounds), cut into pieces

3 quarts water

2 large onions, coarsely chopped

4 sprigs parsley, tied together

1 bay leaf

1 teaspoon salt

1 teaspoon peppercorns, coarsely crushed

5–8 leeks

3 large, or 6 medium, potatoes, peeled and cut into cubes

½ cup half-and-half

freshly grated Parmesan cheese (optional)

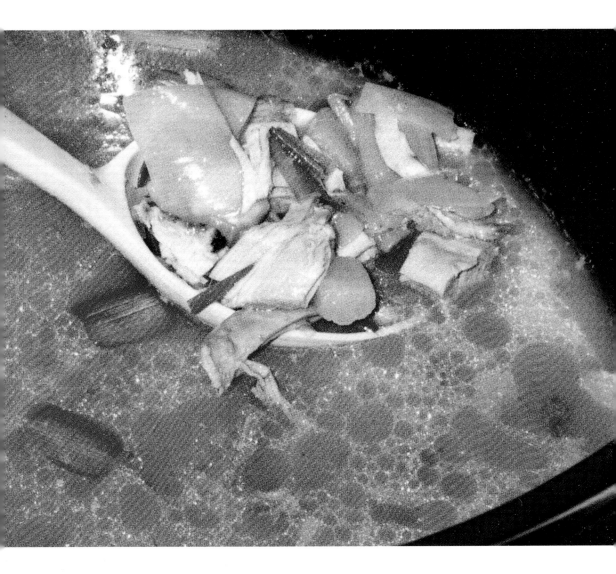

- Put the chicken, water, onions, parsley, bay leaf, salt, and peppercorns in a large stockpot. Bring to a boil, then reduce the heat, cover, and simmer for about 1 hour, until chicken is tender. Remove the chicken from the pot and let cool.

- Split the leeks lengthwise and wash them thoroughly. Cut into 1-inch lengths, using both white and pale green portions. Add to the chicken stock. Add the potatoes. Bring to a gentle boil for 20 minutes, until the leeks and potatoes are tender. Remove the parsley and bay leaf.

- Remove the skin and bones from the chicken. Cut the meat into bite-sized pieces. Add to the soup. Add half-and-half. Heat until the chicken is thoroughly warm, about 3 minutes. Ladle into bowls and sprinkle with Parmesan.

Serves 10 easily.

Turkey

Nearly 300 years ago, the part of North America now known as the United States forfeited almost all of its wild turkeys to the hunter's gun. This bird, once abundant and probably domesticated by pre-Columbian Indians, came close to preceding other New World birds—the passenger pigeon and the Carolina parakeet—into the gaping maw of extinction. To our great good luck, however, the turkey had caught the fancy of the Spanish explorers, who took it home to Spain in the early 1500s. From there, it quickly became popular throughout Europe, not for its meat but for its plumage. And there, in Britain, it received the name by which we know it today. Its Indian name is lost in the mists of pre-history, but *turkey-cock*, the term that the English applied to the guinea fowl of Turkey and other locales in Asia Minor, slipped over onto this fine-feathered New World fowl. When native populations ran perilously low in America, the turkey was reintroduced by European colonists. And just in time, too, for Benjamin Franklin to suggest that it be chosen as the avian representative of the fledgling United States.

In the early 19th century, John James Audubon, writing the bird descriptions that he called "ornithological biography," had this to say about Franklin and his despair that the bald eagle had bumped the turkey aside:

> I grieve that it [the eagle] should have been selected as the emblem of my country. The opinion of our great Franklin on this subject, as it perfectly coincides with mine, I shall here present to you. "For my part," says he, in one of his letters, "I wish the bald eagle had not been chosen as the representative of our country. His is a bird of bad moral character; he does not get his living honestly; you may have seen him perched on some dead tree, where, too lazy to fish for himself, he watches the labour of the Fishing-Hawk; and when that bird has at length taken a fish . . . the Bald Eagle pursues him and takes it from him. With all this injustice, he is never in good case, but, like those among men who live by sharping and robbing, he is generally poor, and often very lousy. Besides, he is a rank coward."

Nonetheless, the bird came close to extinction a second time. It is only in very recent years that wild turkey stocks have recovered from a pitiful low—100,000 birds, all told—at the turn of the 20th century.

Nowadays, the emphasis is on the meat, not the feathers. And a holiday turkey—an everyday turkey, for that matter—can seem as endless to dispose of as a full ham. Sliced turkey, turkey divan, turkey hash . . . the list of possibilities for the leftovers is long (and tedious) indeed. But the end comes eventually, and here are two ways of turning the last of the festive bird into something special.

Franklin's Bird: A Turkey-Vegetable Soup

I do not know if Franklin ever ate turkey soup, though bird soups were not uncommon in his day, but I make bold to suppose that this soup would have delighted his palate.

Variation: A secret ingredient may be added—secret because most people will not be able to guess where the tantalizing sweetness comes from. But you'll know that it's fried onions. To enhance the soup in this way, use 2 diced onions instead of just 1. While the turkey meat and vegetables are simmering, melt 1 tablespoon butter and sauté the second onion until the pieces turn golden. Add the sautéed onion to the soup along with the rice and pasta.

Ingredients

1 turkey carcass, small bones discarded

water to cover

1 large onion, diced

2–3 medium carrots, peeled and diced

1 rib celery, diced

1 small turnip, peeled and diced

1 1-inch wedge green cabbage, chopped

¼ cup black-eyed peas, frozen or canned and drained

leftover turkey meat, cut into bite-sized pieces

leftover turkey gravy and/or stock

½ teaspoon garlic powder

½ teaspoon salt (or to taste)

¼ teaspoon black pepper, freshly ground

1 tablespoon long-grain white rice

2 tablespoons wild rice (optional)

1 scant handful egg noodles

1 scant handful thin spaghetti, broken into 1-inch lengths

- Place the turkey carcass in a large stockpot and cover with water at least an inch over the bones. Simmer, covered, for 1 hour. Remove the bones. Cut off any meat and return it to the pot.

- Add the onion, carrots, celery, turnip, cabbage, black-eyed peas, turkey meat, gravy and/or stock. Simmer for 1 hour more. Add water if needed.

- Put the rice and pasta into the pot and simmer for 30 more minutes. Ladle into bowls.

Serves at least 6 good appetites. Freezes well.

Turkey Soup with Tomatoes, Beans, and Pasta

Ah, turkey soup with an Italian flavor! And easy to boot. This one is best made as a 2-day soup, the first for cooking the turkey stock, the second for adding the other ingredients. The work is hardly onerous. Stock in the making needs to be checked only occasionally to see if more water is needed. On Day II, a mere hour suffices to see onion, garlic, carrots, and the rest lined up on the counter, prepared for the pot, and cooked to sheer deliciousness.

Note: Make this one in a large stockpot, not a 5-quart soup pot.

Day I: The Stock

Ingredients

2½–3 pounds turkey thighs

water to cover by 1 inch

• Place the turkey thighs in a large stockpot. Cover with water. Bring to a boil, then reduce the heat to a simmer and skim off any foam. Continue simmering for 6 to 8 hours. Add water as necessary to keep the turkey covered.

• Remove the turkey from the pot. When it is cool, remove the meat, discarding the skin, fat, and bones. Cut the meat into bite-sized pieces and reserve.

• Meanwhile, pour the stock into a large container and refrigerate overnight. In the morning, remove the fat from the top.

Makes about 10 cups.

Day II: The Soup

Ingredients

2 tablespoons olive oil

1 large onion, chopped

5 large cloves garlic, pressed

10 cups turkey stock

meat from the thighs

1 28-ounce can Italian tomatoes, stewed or diced, with juice

2 carrots, peeled and coarsely grated

2 ribs celery, diced

½ cup small pasta (small shells, orecchiette, orzo)

1 15-ounce can white beans (navy, great northern, cannellini), drained and rinsed

1 teaspoon dried basil

• Heat the oil in a large stockpot over medium heat. Add the onions and garlic; frizzle until the onions are translucent.

• Add the turkey stock, turkey meat, tomatoes, carrots, and celery. Bring to a boil. Reduce the heat and simmer for 10 minutes.

• Add the pasta and beans. Simmer for 10 minutes, or until the pasta is cooked. Ladle into bowls.

Serves at least 8. Freezes well.

Ducks and Geese

Both ducks and geese, wild or tame, may be treated like turkeys. You'll have stock left over from cooking the heart and gizzards and gravy left over from the meal. But because ducks and geese are far more blubbery than turkeys, remove as much of the fat as you possibly can before putting the carcass of a duck or a goose into the soup pot. Then proceed as in the recipe for Franklin's Bird: Turkey Vegetable Soup, page 131.

Pheasant

The ring-necked pheasant is almost ubiquitous coast to coast across the northern tier of the United States. While the female wears feathers of modest, brown-speckled beige, the male is sartorially elegant, from his iridescent purple-green ear tufts and bright red eye patches to the tip of his long black-banded brown tail. The bird's original home was Eurasia, as the scientific name attests: *Phasianus colchicus*, or "pheasant from the Colchis," an ancient land at the end of the Black Sea, which is now part of the Republic of Georgia. Colchis was home to the mythical Medea, who married the Greek Argonaut Jason. As for the pheasant, both male and female are noisy creatures, and the male also delivers a loud, imperious, two-note call—*kok-kak*. I've heard it in the most remote country and also in the shrubbery of Princeton, New Jersey, three blocks from downtown.

Unless you hunt or know a hunter of birds, finding a pheasant can be a thankless task—but for one thing. It is farm-raised to be flushed or retrieved in field trials held for bird dogs like springer spaniels, pointers, and Labrador retrievers. So look for a pheasant farm or a field trial. At either one, you may well luck out.

Pheasant Soup

At the end of the 1960s, on a crisp November day in the western part of Pennsylvania, my daughter and I were spectators at a springer field trial. The birds were selling at day's end for a dollar each, an opportunity that couldn't be passed up. We brought home three. To the detriment of her home-work, my daughter spent the evening plucking and cleaning the birds, but her English teacher gave her an extension on the grounds that he'd never heard a more original excuse for being dilatory. Braised pheasant and pheasant soup, the birds were delicious.

Pheasants are relatively small birds. The soup is cooked with the bones in, but it's not difficult to remove them before serving. The recipe below may easily be doubled or tripled.

Ingredients

2 tablespoons butter

1 pheasant, plucked (or skinned), cleaned, and disjointed

½ cup flour seasoned with salt and pepper

1 medium onion, chopped

3 ribs celery, including some yellow inner leaves, chopped

¼ teaspoon dried thyme

½ teaspoon dried marjoram

1 teaspoon chopped fresh parsley, or ½ teaspoon dried parsley

2 cups chicken stock (see page 179)

½ cup dry red wine

•   Melt the butter over medium-low heat in a large soup pot. Place the pheasant pieces in a bag containing seasoned flour and shake until the pieces are coated well. Then brown them in the butter, turning once, for 3 minutes on each side.

- Add the onion, celery, thyme, marjoram, and parsley. Stir them around in the pot for 3 minutes. Add the stock and wine. Bring to a boil. Reduce the heat, cover, and simmer for 1½ hours, until the meat is falling off the bones.

- Remove the pheasant pieces from the pot. Discard the bones and return the meat to the pot. Bring the pot to a gentle boil before turning off the heat and ladling the soup into bowls.

Serves 2. Freezes well.

Chapter Five
Soups from the Sea

Up to this chapter, I've dealt with long-domesticated plants and animals. But the denizens of the world's waters remain wild. Yes, there are farms that raise fish, shrimp, crawfish, and other marine creatures, but in the fashion of the hunter-gatherers that all of us were once upon a time, we still must hunt for most of our seafood. Fishing boats go out on trawling expeditions, gill and pound nets are set, lobster traps and crab pots fitted with buoys are dropped into the briny. Fish, shellfish, crustaceans, algae—both salt water and fresh water abound in good things to eat. These days, the catch is never assured but depends on weather, the presence or absence of food supplies for the prey species, the strength or weakness of marine populations, and government regulation. But thanks to persistent fishermen, our seafood and supermarkets display an imposing array, ranging from finny swimmers to scallops and clams, shrimp, and crabs. All make scrumptious soups.

Fish Soups

My husband, the Chief, and I do considerable fishing, setting a gill net right off our seawall in North Carolina's wide and salty River Neuse. Summer mornings and evenings, with a cooler roped to my waist, I wade in, extracting the fish and, sometimes, the blue crabs that have tangled themselves in the meshes. Bluefish, flounder, jumping mullet, spot, croaker, red drum, Spanish mackerel, and more—a summer's worth of fishing fills the freezer for the rest of the year. When I married him, willy-nilly, I became a woman covered with fish scales—a veritable fishwife, but he says, "No, hon, a mermaid." We have no trouble disposing of every last bit of the catch. Some of it lands, of course, in the soup.

Puppy Drum Stew: A Fish Chowder, North Carolina Style

What is puppy drum? Formally, it's *Sciaenops ocellatus*, a member of the drum family, which includes black drum, spotted seatrout, gray trout (or weakfish), croaker, and spot. Most people, naturally choosing informality, call it redfish (as in blackened redfish), channel bass, or red drum. *Puppy* refers to the small, juvenile version of a fish that can grow to 60 pounds or more, with scales that need to be scraped off with a hoe. Young or mature, it's a handsome fish with silvery scales that hold a glint of copper. It sports a dark copper-ringed eye spot—sometimes more than one—just aft of its caudal fin. This spot, or ocellation, fools predators into thinking that they're nipping at heads when they are really only tweaking tails. The minimum length at which a puppy drum may be taken is 18 inches. I've been lucky enough to have some that size swim into my crab pots in hot pursuit of a crustacean dinner. There, trapped, they become our dinner.

Drum has firm flesh that is supremely right for making fish stew, a dish that nonsoutherners would call chowder.

Carolinians sometimes use flounder as the fish in puppy drum stew. Striped mullet is another, though not traditional, choice. If you can't find the species mentioned here, any firm-fleshed fish, like cod, red snapper, or haddock, will do, be it whole or filleted. I prefer fish with the bones in, for cooking these, along with the flesh, adds gelatin to the mixture. There's no such thing as too many onions; use more than 5, if you'd like.

And here's a variation that provides an extra treat:

- Poach eggs in the stew—a few or enough to cover the top—just before serving.

Ingredients

1 puppy drum of at least the legal length

water enough to poach or steam the fish

6 slices bacon, or a chunk of meaty salt pork cut into small cubes

5 large onions, diced

3 medium potatoes, cut into 1/2-inch cubes

½ cup whole milk (optional)

1 tablespoon butter (optional)

salt and pepper to taste

• Steam or poach the puppy drum on a rack inside a stockpot until the flesh flakes easily. Remove the fish and place it on a platter. Reserve the liquid in which the fish was cooked. Remove the fish's skin and bones and discard them. Reserve the meat.

• In a skillet, frizzle the bacon or salt pork until crisp and set it aside. Pour off all but 2 tablespoons of fat. Sauté the onions until translucent, about 5 minutes.

• As the onions sauté, put the potatoes into the liquid reserved from cooking the fish and boil them for 15 minutes. Add the fish and onions. Add the milk and butter, if you'd like. When the butter has melted, add the salt pork or crumbled bacon to the pot. Simmer for a few minutes until heated through. Season to taste and serve piping hot.

Serves 6 hearty appetites, 8 that are more restrained.
Freezes well for up to two months.

Fish Soup with Tomatoes

Many fish soups are chowder-white, but here's one that's tomato-red and mildly spicy—yum! Not many cookbooks specify tomatoes as a prime ingredient in fish soup, so this soup sprang from my experience somewhat like Aphrodite springing from the sea. The turmeric adds little flavor to the soup but does impart its glowing golden color to the tomatoes and the stock. When it comes to stock, that made from fish is superior, but chicken stock may be substituted. The whole works takes little more than an hour to prepare from chopping the vegetables through adding the fish to ladling the scrumptious results into a bowl.

Note: Make this one in a large stockpot, not a 5-quart soup pot.

Ingredients

2 tablespoons olive oil

2 medium onions, finely diced

2 large cloves garlic, pressed

1 large leek, finely chopped

3 ribs celery, including some yellow inner leaves, finely chopped

1 teaspoon turmeric

1 dried cayenne pepper, crumbled, or ¼ teaspoon red pepper flakes

½ teaspoon dried thyme

1 bay leaf

2 14½-ounce cans crushed tomatoes

6 cups fish stock (see page 182)

1 cup dry white wine

salt and pepper to taste

2 medium potatoes, peeled and cut into ½-inch cubes

2 pounds nonoily fish (cod, rockfish, red snapper, others), cut into 1-inch chunks

2 tablespoons minced fresh parsley

- Heat the oil in a large stockpot over medium heat. Add the onions and garlic; sauté until the onions are translucent, about 5 minutes. Add the leek and celery; sauté for 5 minutes more.

- Stir in the turmeric, cayenne pepper, thyme, bay leaf, tomatoes, fish stock, wine, and salt and pepper. Bring to a boil. Add the potatoes and cook at a gentle boil for 20 minutes, or until potatoes are cooked through.

- Add the fish. Continue cooking for 5 minutes, or until fish is white and flaky. Sprinkle parsley atop soup. Ladle into bowls.

Serves 6 easily. Freezes well.

Fish Bisque with Mushrooms

Once upon a time, bisques were made of boiled-down birds or crawfish. Today, the word specifically designates a creamy soup containing shellfish or crustaceans. But fish are denizens of the sea as well, and I have found that fish bisque is not only possible but delicious. Because of the bright red and green bell peppers that simmer in its thick and creamy white liquid, I think of this one as Christmas Soup. And we have indeed served it as the soup course of a Christmas Eve buffet supper. The menu was posted for all to see. I just did not tell anyone what kind of fish I'd used until the soup was gone: cow-nosed stingray—in particular, the firm, delicious flesh of its wings. One summer on the Carolina coast, hearing that stingray was not only edible but tasted like scallops, I collected one from a neighbor who'd found several entangled in his gill net, and I filleted the wings. Scallops? No, the fillets, dark meat striated like cube steaks, are not so chewy as scallops. Instead, they taste as fresh and sweet as frogs' legs.

No need, however, to seek out stingray for this recipe, which is prepared in a heavy-duty 12-inch skillet. As with puppy drum stew, any fish with firm flesh will suffice, be it striped bass, red snapper, or cod.

Ingredients

3 tablespoons butter

1 small onion, diced

1 clove garlic, pressed

$\frac{1}{2}$ cup thin-sliced mushrooms

$\frac{1}{4}$ cup diced green bell pepper

$\frac{1}{4}$ cup diced red bell pepper

2 tablespoons flour

1 cup milk

1 cup half-and-half

$1\frac{1}{2}$ pounds boneless fish

½ cup dry white wine

salt and pepper to taste

- Melt the butter in a skillet. Sauté the onion, garlic, mushrooms, and green and red peppers until the onion is translucent and the mushrooms are cooked, about 5 minutes. Add the flour; heat and stir until bubbly. Mix the milk and half-and-half, and add them gradually, stirring all the while.

- Mix in the fish and simmer until the flesh flakes, about 15 minutes.

- Add the wine and simmer for another 15 minutes. Season to taste.

Serves 6. Freezes well.

Deep-Sea Chowder

Chowder—that bluff, no-nonsense word comes from Latin by way of French. *Calderia* is Latin for "cauldron" or "kettle" and, by extension, for the kettle's contents. Softening the hard *c*, French tongues came up with *chaudriére*. English speakers proceeded to reinstall the blunt sounds of the ancestral word. In the beginning, all manner of edibles comprised a chowder, but the word has become restricted to soups and stews in which seafood—clams, mussels, fish—is the primary ingredient. Yes, there are corn and other vegetable chowders, which are put together like the canonical chowder, except that they lack the seafood.

Pat Schrishuhn's chowder has a fillip: It features elbow macaroni instead of potatoes. As it simmers, its aromas— bacon, onion, garlic, thyme, fish—fill the kitchen with the most enticing smells. Luckily, it's quick and easy to make. Start at 10:30 A.M., finish by noon in time for lunch.

Ingredients

1½ cups elbow macaroni

4 slices bacon, cut into 1-inch pieces

1 cup chopped onion

1 cup chopped celery

½ cup chopped celery leaves

½ cup chopped fresh parsley

1 clove garlic, minced

2 8-ounce cans minced clams

1 teaspoon salt

½ teaspoon dried thyme

¾ teaspoon black pepper, freshly ground

1 bay leaf

2 12-ounce cans evaporated milk

1 pound filleted nonoily fish (such as cod, bass, red snapper), cut into cubes

⅓ cup flour

⅓ cup water

grated Parmesan cheese

- Cook the macaroni al dente. Reserve.

- Fry the bacon pieces in a large soup pot until partially cooked. Add the onion, celery, celery leaves, parsley, and garlic. Cook over medium heat until the onion is translucent, about 10 minutes.

- Drain the clams, reserving the liquid. Add water to make 4 cups liquid. Put into the soup pot along with the salt, thyme, pepper, and bay leaf. Bring to a boil. Reduce the heat, cover, and simmer for 10 minutes.

- Add the evaporated milk, macaroni, clams, and fish. Bring to a boil. Reduce the heat and simmer gently for 15 minutes.

- Blend the flour with the water until smooth. Add to the soup and cook over medium heat, stirring, until smooth. Correct the seasoning. Serve in large deep soup bowls and garnish with Parmesan cheese.

Serves 8. Freezes well.

Portuguese Seafood Soup

The recipe comes from my friend and onetime college roommate Shay Edwards. She in turn acquired it from a Brazilian composer friend and traveling companion. Making the soup at first presented me with problems. I live for part of the year in the landlocked Shenandoah Valley, where seafood markets are few and far between. Fresh shellfish like clams and scallops are not easy to come by. Indeed, they're well nigh impossible to obtain. Luckily, frozen scallops may be found in the seafood department of many supermarkets. The only clams to be had, however, are those that come in cans.

I asked Shay if it would be all right to substitute canned (rubber) clams for the cherrystones called for in the recipe. Her answer was firm: No, it would not. But she took great pity on my clamless state and shipped me not only the cherrystones but also the shrimp, scallops, and fish. The shrimp were a tiny variety that Carolinians would call popcorn or Calabash shrimp.

The secret of the soup's flavor—indeed, its very soul—is the cherrystone clam, *Mercenaria mercenaria*, which may be translated as "reward reward." It's also known as the northern quahog, a name formed from the Native word for this shellfish that the Narragansett Indians introduced to European colonists. And a reward twice over it most certainly is.

For you who live lamentably far from fresh seafood, here's the address of a market that delivers everything from fish to clams (three varieties) to shrimp and live lobsters anywhere in the United States: Falmouth Fish Market, Inc., 157/159 Teaticket Highway, East Falmouth, Massachusetts 02536. The toll-free telephone number is 1-800-628-0045.

The soup is quick and easy to make, taking no more than an hour and a half from the dicing of the vegetables to adding salt and pepper at the end. Two methods of making it are given below, one in which shrimp create their own broth, another that uses shrimp broth already made.

Of this special treat from the sea, Shay says, "It's one of my favorites. A loaf of crusty bread, a bottle of white wine, and a big salad makes company fare. Purr!"

Method I

Ingredients

½ pound small shrimp

3 cups water

3 tablespoons olive oil

1 medium onion, finely diced

3 carrots, peeled and finely diced

4 large tomatoes, peeled and finely chopped, or 1 cup tomato puree

1 8-ounce bottle clam juice

1 14½-ounce can chicken broth

1 pound cherrystone clams, scrubbed

½ pound scallops

1 pound ocean catfish or scrod (young cod), cut into 1½-inch chunks

½ cup dry white wine

1 clove garlic, pressed

½ teaspoon dried basil

1 teaspoon cumin

salt and pepper to taste

1 lemon, sliced thin

• Boil the shrimp in the water until pink. Remove the shrimp; reserve the water. Cool the shrimp and remove their shells. Return the shells to the water and simmer for 15 minutes. Then strain the water to remove the shells. Reserve the shrimp broth.

• Meanwhile, heat the olive oil in a large soup pot and sauté the onion and carrots until the onion is translucent, about 5 minutes. Add the tomatoes or tomato puree, clam juice, chicken broth, and shrimp broth to the onion-carrot sauté. Bring to a simmer. Add the clams and simmer until they open, about 15 minutes. Keep the simmer going; stir in the scallops and fish. Add the wine, garlic, basil, cumin, and salt and pepper to taste. Stir in the cooked shrimp. Simmer just until the shrimp are heated through.

- Float a thin slice of lemon on each serving.

Serves 6. Freezes well indeed.

Method II

Ingredients

3 tablespoons olive oil

1 onion, finely diced

3 carrots, finely diced

4 large tomatoes, peeled and finely chopped, or 1 cup tomato puree

1 8-ounce bottle clam juice

1 14$\frac{1}{2}$-ounce can chicken broth

3 cups shrimp broth (see page 183)

1 pound cherrystone clams

$\frac{1}{2}$ pound small shrimp, shelled

$\frac{1}{2}$ pound scallops

1 pound ocean catfish or scrod (young cod), cut into 1$\frac{1}{2}$-inch chunks

$\frac{1}{2}$ cup dry white wine

1 clove garlic, pressed

½ teaspoon dried basil

1 teaspoon cumin

salt and pepper to taste

1 lemon, sliced thin

- Heat the olive oil in a large soup pot and sauté the onion and carrots until the onion is translucent, about 5 minutes. Add the tomatoes or tomato puree, clam juice, chicken broth, and shrimp broth to the onion-carrot sauté. Bring to a simmer. Add the clams and simmer until they open, about 15 minutes. Keep the simmer going; stir in the shrimp, scallops, and fish. Add the wine, garlic, basil, cumin, and salt and pepper to taste. Simmer for 5 minutes. Ladle into bowls.

- Float a thin slice of lemon on each serving.

Serves 6. Freezes very well.

Cioppino

Cioppino is said to be a specialty of San Francisco, but you can be sure that it descends from Italy in both name and ingredients. *Ciuppin* is a Genoese word for this sort of concoction. I've heard it said that cioppino is the Italian equivalent of French bouillabaisse, a hearty soup that uses the best of the day's catch of fish. But a traditional bouillabaisse uses fish and only fish (though lobsters have been known to be thrown in the pot), while cioppino is all-embracing, finding its flavor in a combination of fish, shellfish, and crustaceans, all simmered in a tomato sauce rich with herbs and spices.

Recipes for cioppino are as many as fish in the ocean. The one below is my amalgam of the basic fish-shellfish-crustacean-tomato idea with the herbs and spices I like best. The fragrance of onion, bell pepper, and fennel seeds as they sauté has more allure for me than any perfume. I had the pleasure, too, of using meat from fish and crabs that I had caught and shrimp that were bought right off a coastal trawler. For this soup, I also chose the easy route, using canned tomatoes and clams, as well as bottled clam juice. The soup is fail-safe in its preparation and ranks high on the quick-and-easy list.

And it begs for creativity:

- Combine your favorite herbs and spices along with the mandatory basil and oregano.
- Puree flavored diced tomatoes—those with jalapeño peppers or mild green chilies—and use them instead of plain old crushed tomatoes. (If you use the jalapeño variety, omit the hot red pepper.)
- Go wild with seafood. Add mussels and/or scallops, find fresh cherrystone clams, plop live hard-shelled crabs in the pot, use the cooked meat of a lobster tail.

Ingredients

⅓ cup olive oil

2 large onions, chopped

2 ribs celery, chopped

1 green bell pepper, seeded and chopped

6 cloves garlic, chopped

½ cup minced fresh parsley

1 teaspoon fennel seeds

1 28-ounce can crushed tomatoes

¼ teaspoon dried thyme

½ teaspoon dried rosemary

dash of cinnamon

1 bay leaf

1 dried cayenne pepper, crumbled, or ½ teaspoon hot red pepper flakes

2 6½-ounce cans diced clams, juices reserved

2 8-ounce bottles clam juice

1 cup dry red wine

1 tablespoon red wine vinegar

1 pound nonoily fish (cod, rockfish, red snapper, others), cut into 1-inch pieces

1 pound shrimp, shelled and deveined

8 ounces cooked crabmeat

- Heat the oil in a large soup pot over medium heat. Add the onions, celery, bell pepper, garlic, parsley, and fennel seeds, and sauté until the onions are translucent, about 8 minutes. (Enjoy the fragrance.)

- Add the tomatoes. Bring to a boil. Reduce the heat and simmer for 10 minutes.

- Add the thyme, rosemary, cinnamon, bay leaf, cayenne pepper, clams, clam juice, wine, and wine vinegar. Simmer for 30 minutes.

- Stir in the fish and shrimp. Bring to a boil. Reduce the heat and cook for 2 minutes, until the shrimp are pink.

- Add the crabmeat and cook until heated through.

Serves 6. Freezes well.

Crabs

Callinectes sapidus—that's the formal name of the blue crab. It means "beautiful swimmer that's tasty." I spend much of my summer in pursuit of these truly tasty crustaceans—setting and fishing crab pots in North Carolina's wide and salty River Neuse, cleaning the catch, picking out the sweet white meat, and playing with recipes from crab cakes to crab soups. And here are three of the latter. The first two are skillet soups.

Caution: If you use store-bought crabmeat for any recipe featuring this succulent crustacean, be sure to pick through it carefully to remove any lingering shards of shell.

Crab Jambalaya

Jambalayas come from Louisiana. There's some argument about the origin of the name, however. Some people have it that *jambalaya* is a legacy from the days that the Spanish held sway in that part of the world and was formed from the Spanish word *jamón*, which means "ham." It more closely resembles a French word for ham, *jambon*. But both *Webster's Third International Dictionary* and the *Oxford English Dictionary* (my favorite) say that it was taken directly from the Provençal term *jambalaia*, refer-

ring to a thick concoction of rice and fowl. The last strikes me as being by far the most likely. Nonetheless, ham usually graces a classic jambalaya.

These days, jambalaya, thick as a stew and occurring in many versions, features ham, seafood, tomatoes, and rice. In the recipe below, ham takes the form of bacon. The soup is easy to make, taking only 45 minutes from start to finish. If extra liquid is needed (rice is thirsty stuff), add just enough tomato juice, V-8, or Clamato—the last is especially good—to keep the soup from sticking to the bottom of the pot while retaining its thick texture. The recipe may easily be doubled.

Ingredients

6 slices bacon

1 medium onion, diced

2 cloves garlic, minced

1 rib celery, diced

¼ cup chopped green bell pepper

2 14½-ounce cans diced tomatoes

¼ cup uncooked long-grain white rice (not instant)

1 cup crabmeat

1 teaspoon Worcestershire sauce

1 tablespoon dry sherry

- Fry the bacon crisp in a heavy-duty 12-inch skillet. Set it aside. Pour off all but 2 tablespoons of the bacon drippings.

- Sauté the onion, garlic, celery, and green pepper in the drippings for 5 minutes. Add the tomatoes, undrained, and rice. Simmer until the rice is tender, stirring occasionally, for about 20 to 25 minutes.

- Stir in the crabmeat, Worcestershire sauce, and sherry. Heat through. Ladle into bowls and top with crumbled bacon.

Variations: Use shrimp, shelled and cleaned, instead of crab. Add them to the jambalaya with the Worcestershire sauce and sherry, and cook until the shrimp turn pink, about 3 minutes. If you double the recipe, use both crab and shrimp.

Serves 4. Freezes well.

She-Crab Bisque

Here's a crab delight, a true bisque that features the meat and bright orange roe of a female crab, called a "jenny" in coastal North Carolina, a "sook" in the Chesapeake. Some cookbooks have it that roe crabs are not legal to catch. But in coastal Carolina, it is legal to take them if they meet two criteria: Their shells must meet the mandatory minimum length of 5 inches measured spine to spine, and they must not have reached the sponge state, in which eggs, about to hatch, force open the apron on their mother's abdomen and protrude like a hard brownish ball. That is, if her eggs are visible, the crab must be sent home to the water. If not, she may be kept and her roe saved along with the meat.

It's not always possible to obtain crab roe. To make up for the lack, some cooks put the crumbled yolks of hard-boiled eggs in the bottom of bowls just before serving and cover them with soup. For this recipe, two egg yolks suffice.

Because of the half-and-half, the soup is extraordinarily rich. If you'd like to cut back a little, use only 2 cups half-and-half and 2 cups milk.

Serve this soup with saltwater corn cakes (page 188).

Ingredients

¼ cup butter (no substitute)

1 small onion, diced fine

½ teaspoon freshly grated lemon zest

2 tablespoons flour

4 cups half-and-half

1 pound crabmeat and roe

½ cup dry sherry

1 teaspoon Worcestershire sauce

pinch of nutmeg

salt and pepper to taste

- Melt the butter in a heavy-duty 12-inch skillet. Sauté the onion and zest for about 5 minutes. Add the flour; heat and stir until bubbly. Gradually add the half-and-half.

- Mix in the crabmeat and roe, and simmer for 30 minutes.

- Add the sherry, Worcestershire sauce, and nutmeg, and simmer for another 15 minutes. Season to taste.

Serves 4 hearty appetites or 6 that are more modest.

Land and Sea Crab Soup

Once upon a time, a commercial soup company (I cannot remember its name) offered a canned Maryland crab soup—crabmeat swimming with carrots, peas, and beans in a tomatoey broth. Combining some of the best of the sea with the best of the earth, it was ineluctably good. Along with cheese, crackers, and fruit, it was a lunchtime treat. But I haven't seen it on supermarket shelves for years. The recipe below suggests, rather than re-creates, that long-lost soup. I have a sneaking suspicion that it may also be better on two counts than the one I remember with great fondness: It is not canned, and it contains more, much more, crab.

It is, however, made with some frozen vegetables. Fresh ones may replace them, of course; they just take longer to prepare. If you opt for fresh ingredients, use them in the same proportions as the frozen kind.

Ingredients

2 tablespoons olive oil

1 large onion, diced

2 ribs celery, diced

4 cups vegetable stock (see page 175)

3 cups tomato juice or V-8

½ cup dry red wine

1 large potato, peeled and cut into ½-inch cubes

1 carrot, finely diced

½ teaspoon dried thyme

1 teaspoon salt

¼ teaspoon pepper

½ cup frozen peas

½ cup frozen baby limas

½ cup frozen green beans

8 ounces crabmeat

- Heat the oil in a large soup pot. Sauté the onion and celery in oil until the onion is translucent.

- Add the vegetable stock, tomato juice, wine, potato, carrot, thyme, salt, and pepper. Bring to a boil, cover, and simmer for 15 minutes, until the potato is barely tender.

- Add the frozen peas, limas, and green beans. Simmer for 15 minutes.

- Add the crabmeat, cooking only until it is warmed through.

Serves 6 if ladled into bowls, and 8 if into cups. Best not to freeze.

Shrimp

Every summer, in late July or early August, I load two 48-quart coolers in the car and drive 20 miles to a dock on the Atlantic Intracoastal Waterway. The purpose: to meet the shrimp trawlers as they're unloading and to bring home 50 pounds of truly fresh shrimp. They have a salty-sweet taste that can't be bought at a supermarket fish counter and, often, not at a fish market either. I spend the rest of the day heading and packaging the critters, which range in size from large to jumbo. A pint freezer bag holds a pound. When I'm done, our year's supply has been put in.

What are shrimp anyway? They're crustaceans related to crabs, lobsters, and crawfish. And they come in some 2,000 species, all of which belong to the suborder Natantia, the "swimmers." Some are 8 inches long; others, like brine shrimp, are so small that you can barely see them. Not all of them are edible. The trawlers on the Carolina coast are pulling their nets to catch the succulent white, pink, and brown shrimp of the genus *Peneus*. In Greek myth, Peneus was god of the river that bore his name, and he fathered the nymph Daphne, who escaped an assault by Apollo when Earth took pity and transformed her into the world's first bay laurel. (So, because her leaves impart noble flavor, Daphne, along with her father, gives virtue to cooking.) It seems appropriate that the scientific name for shrimp honors the realm of water.

And the word *shrimp* comes from the Germanic side of English. It began with an old verb meaning "to shrink up" and eventually came to refer to something little, in this case a creature small in size— but huge in flavor.

But soup is the order of the day, and here are two that put shrimp in the bowl.

Spicy Shrimp and Corn Chowder

Carol Kidd is a retired science teacher with sparkly eyes and snow-white hair. She's also an ardent golfer and a master gardener. Of her soup cookery, she says this: "I first decided to learn to make soup when I inherited a teacup collection from my mother-in-law. I believe that if you have nice things, you should use them. Therefore, my teacups had to be used. Formal teas don't regularly fit into our lifestyle, so I decided to serve soup in them. This spicy chowder is one of my more successful attempts."

It succeeds very well indeed. And it is the only soup in this book that is baked—yes, *baked*. The soup may be made in two parts—through the food-mill stage on one day and the baking stage on the next. But there's really no need to stretch out the procedure, for the soup pot's contents may be quickly cooled by immersing the pot in cold water and stirring out the heat before processing everything in a food mill. Carol's special instructions are placed in quotation marks below.

First, here's my own fillip to Carol's basic recipe—an addition that just plain agrees with chowder of every sort:

- Frizzle 4 to 6 slices of bacon as the chowder bakes. Drain and reserve. When the chowder is ready, crumble them and sprinkle them atop the soup.

Note: Make this one in a large stockpot, not a 5-quart soup pot.

Ingredients

1 tablespoon butter

1 large onion, diced

1–4 crumbled dried hot peppers, including seeds ("number of peppers to taste"), or

½–2 teaspoons red pepper flakes

8 cups chicken stock (see page 179)

2 to 3 medium russet potatoes, peeled and cut into 1-inch cubes

2 14¾-ounce cans cream-style corn

1 pound shrimp, shelled, deveined, and split lengthwise

1 11-ounce can white shoepeg corn

1 12-ounce can evaporated milk, or 1½ cups heavy cream

1 2-ounce jar diced pimientos, drained and rinsed

salt and pepper to taste

- Place the butter, onion, and red pepper in a large stockpot and cook over low heat until the onion is translucent, about 5 minutes.

- Add the chicken stock, potatoes, and cream-style corn. Bring to a boil. Reduce the heat and "simmer until potatoes have rounded edges," about 30 minutes.

- Cool the ingredients to room temperature (give the pot a cold-water bath). Then put them through a food mill. ("Blender or food processor will produce sharp edges on corn—unpleasant in the throat. So do not use.") Return the milled ingredients to the soup pot. ("Soup may be put aside at this point," refrigerated, and continued the next day.)

- Preheat the oven to 400⁻ Fahrenheit.

- Add the shrimp, shoepeg corn, evaporated milk or cream, and pimientos to the pot. "Heat in the oven until shrimp are spiraled and pink, and the soup is steaming, stirring occasionally," for 15 minutes, or 30 minutes if the soup has gone into the oven cold. Adjust the seasonings. Ladle into bowls.

Serves 6 hearty appetites, 8 that are more restrained.

Shrimp Filé Gumbo

Jambalaya, a crawfish pie, and a filé gumbo, for tonight I'm gonna see my m'chere mio—so goes the Cajun song that was a hit in the late 1940s. Crawfish pie isn't soup; jambalaya has had its turn in the section on crab soups. And here's the filé gumbo, a Creole soup born in Louisiana of culinary ecumenism, for it contains elements from African, European, and Native American cuisine. This particular filé gumbo is the real thing, a double-barreled soup that uses both of the traditional thickeners—finely powdered sassafras leaves and okra. The first is filé; the second, gumbo, which is the Bantu name for okra (itself a West African word for the plant). I'm lucky enough to be able to make my own filé powder by drying sassafras leaves, then grinding them fine. The stuff is more readily available in the Cajun section of many supermarkets. Both thickeners work by adding a glutinous smoothness to the liquid.

Many cookbooks, however, forbid combining the two in a single soup. The reason: One is enough, but both together make for a consistency akin to that of glue. The books also interdict the use of filé powder until the very last moment, when the heat is turned off, lest it form unattractive strings in the soup. No, not so! There are two secrets to the cooking:

- Using whole, rather than cut, okra keeps its jellylike substance inside until you bite into it.
- Then, if you whisk in the filé powder while the soup is cooking, and keep whisking, you'll find nary a string. The consistency will be like velvet. (Credit where credit's due: I learned this trick from food writer Barbara Kafka in her compendious book *Soup: A Way of Life*.)

Another secret is that you can create your own shrimp stock on the spot. Canned chicken broth can be utterly transformed when shrimp shells are simmered in it.

Like all gumbos, this one is labor intensive (though it takes only 2 hours to make). You stir and stir and keep on stirring. But, oh, the flavor is worth it. Serve it in a bowl or over a mound of rice on a plate.

Ingredients

1 pound shrimp, shelled and deveined, with shells reserved

6 cups shrimp stock or chicken broth (see pages 183 and 179)

1 large onion, chopped

1 rib celery, chopped

½ cup yellow celery leaves, chopped

6 cloves garlic, chopped

1 dried cayenne pepper, crumbled, or ¼ teaspoon red pepper flakes

¼ teaspoon dried thyme

¼ cup chopped fresh parsley

¼ cup butter

¼ cup flour

1 10-ounce box frozen whole okra

1 teaspoon filé powder

1 tablespoon fresh lemon juice

salt and pepper to taste

hot sauce to taste

2 cups cooked rice

• Put the shrimp shells into the stock and bring to a boil. Reduce the heat and simmer, partly covered, for 30 minutes. Turn off the heat.

• Meanwhile, prepare the onion, celery, celery leaves, garlic, and cayenne pepper, and put them into a bowl. Add the thyme and parsley.

• Melt the butter over medium heat in a large soup pot, and stir in the flour. Keep stirring over medium heat until the roux becomes a light gold-brown, about 5 minutes. Reduce the heat to low and stir constantly until the roux takes on a rich caramel color, about 20 to 25 minutes.

• Increase the heat to medium. Stir in the onion, celery, celery leaves, garlic, cayenne pepper, thyme, and parsley. Cook, stirring frequently, for 10 minutes. Stir in the okra and filé powder. Slowly whisk in the stock. Bring to a boil, whisking frequently. Reduce the heat and simmer for 5 minutes.

• Add the shrimp. Return to a boil. Reduce the heat and simmer for 1 to 2 minutes. Stir in the lemon juice, salt and pepper, and hot sauce. Mix in the rice. Ladle into bowls.

Serves 6. Freezes well.

Chapter Six
Down to Basics: Making Your Own Stock

Stock isn't soup all by itself. It's rather a liquid medium for meat, seafood, and vegetables, which are at home there as fish are at home in the sea. And it may be made in many varieties—chicken, turkey, beef, seafood, vegetable, and others—according to the kind of ingredients that it will surround. Not all soups require stock, of course. For many, like those prepared from dried beans, water does very well indeed. But if you're making, say, a chicken soup or a fish chowder, you can also make a well-seasoned stock better than any canned broth found on a supermarket shelf.

Here, then, are seven down-to-basics recipes. For all of them, begin by bringing the ingredients to a rolling boil, then reduce the heat immediately so that the stock simmers. With proper simmering, the stock seems to go to sleep, breathing only tiny, steady bubbles. Each recipe may be made, of course, in a quantity greater than that specified. The rule of thumb is that stock may be used immediately, stored in the refrigerator for 3 days, or frozen till kingdom come. When turned to ice, it lasts indefinitely.

Tip: Stock can be rapidly cooled after it's strained by putting it back in the stockpot and putting the pot into a bath of cold water. This cooling will help solidify the fat so that it may skimmed off. Or after it has cooled naturally, stock may be refrigerated overnight and the fat removed come morning.

Vegetable Stock

The easiest way to make vegetable stock is simply to save the water in which fresh or frozen vegetables have been cooked. Pour it off into a jar, store it in the refrigerator, and add to it every time you cook veggies. It may also be put directly into the freezer, a little at a time. Let the cooking water cool, and pour it over the already frozen stock. A caution: Don't save the juices from canned vegetables, for they taste—well, canned.

Here's another method for making stock from the good stuff that James Joyce called "weggiebobbles." The ingredients may be varied according to your own taste or, perhaps, to what's available in the refrigerator as well as in the potato and onion bin. No need to peel the vegetables, for their skins add color and nutrients.

Ingredients

12 cups water

1 large onion with skin, coarsely chopped

2 leeks (white part only), washed well and sliced into ½-inch rounds

1 carrot, sliced into 1-inch rounds

1 turnip, cut into ½-inch cubes

1 rib celery, sliced

scant handful yellow celery leaves (not green ones)

1 small zucchini or yellow crookneck squash, sliced

6 outer leaves romaine lettuce, coarsely chopped

½ pound mushrooms, coarsely chopped

1 teaspoon orange zest

2 bay leaves

8 peppercorns

salt to taste

- Pour the water into a stockpot and add all the other ingredients. Bring to a rolling boil. Reduce the heat to medium low and let simmer, uncovered, for 30 minutes, stirring occasionally.

- Cover the pot and let the ingredients simmer for 2 hours.

- Strain the broth through cheesecloth, pressing on the solids with a spoon to extract as much flavor as possible. Let cool, then store in the refrigerator, or freeze to be used when soup hunger strikes.

Makes about 6 cups.

Beef Stock

This uncomplicated method of making beef stock produces a liquid that tastes good all by itself. Beef bones, available at the supermarket meat counter, can be cut there into 2- to 3-inch lengths. Some will have marrow, some won't. At home, they can be frozen until they're needed. Initial preparation of the stock is quick, for all the vegetables are cut into pieces but not peeled. And the meat can be recycled in soup or hash. The stock may be refrigerated for use within 3 days or frozen till kingdom come.

Ingredients

3 pounds beef bones, including marrowbones

1½ pounds beef chuck, cut into quarters

3 quarts water

1 teaspoon salt

8 peppercorns

1 large onion, unpeeled, studded with 4 or 5 cloves

2 carrots, cut into chunks

2 celery ribs, cut into pieces

1 turnip, quartered

2 tomatoes, quartered

2 small leeks

2 sprigs parsley

1 bay leaf

½ teaspoon dried thyme

- Place the bones in boiling water to cover. Cook for 5 minutes and drain well.

- Place the bones and meat in a large soup pot. Add the water. Bring to a rolling boil, then reduce the heat. Skim off foam and fat. Continue to skim until the foam ceases to appear.

- Add the salt, peppercorns, onion, carrots, celery, turnip, tomatoes, leeks, parsley, bay leaf, and thyme. Cover partly and simmer gently for 4 to 5 hours.

- Remove the bones and vegetables. Strain through cheesecloth. Return the stock to the pot and cool quickly by placing the pot in cold water. Refrigerate overnight, and remove solidified fat in the morning (or afternoon, as the case may be).

- Refrigerate for use within 3 days or freeze.

Makes about 10 cups.

Chicken Stock

Chicken stock may be most easily prepared by using only bony chicken parts, like backs, necks, and wings, plus water. I use wings, for it's hard to get the other parts in sufficient quantity. Giblets can be tossed in, too, though not the liver. The stock's potency depends on how long it's simmered—anywhere from 3 hours to a full 12. The longer it cooks, the more the bones will separate, and the more gelatinous the stock will be.

But if you'd like to add vegetables and spices, add them for the last hour of cooking so that they can be used in soup rather than reduced to mush. These vegetables and spices are suitable:

- a peeled onion studded with 6 cloves
- a carrot
- the white and pale green parts of a leek or two
- a rib of celery
- 2 or 3 garlic cloves
- 2 allspice berries
- peppercorns to taste

Save the meat to use immediately, refrigerate for 2 or 3 days, or freeze for a month. It's great in soups like Chicken and Rice (page 113) and Chicken Noodle Picante (page 116).

Ingredients

4 pounds chicken backs, necks, and/or wings

14 cups water

- Place the chicken parts and water in a stockpot and bring to a rolling boil. Reduce the heat and simmer gently for 3 to 12 hours. Skim off fat and froth as necessary.

- Cool to room temperature, and skim off as much fat as possible. Strain through cheesecloth or a fine sieve. Refrigerate for 3 hours to overnight. Remove the solidified fat. Then eat on the spot, store in the fridge, or freeze, as you wish.

Makes about 12 cups.

Bird Stock

This stock is the easiest of all and it may be made from chicken, turkey, duck, or goose. Its uses are many, from the first go-around on the bird to the last. As the bird roasts, the stock simmers, and when the bird is done, the stock is ready to be converted, with drippings and flour, into gravy. Later, it may be a prime ingredient in the cream sauce for, say, turkey or duck hash or chicken à la king. Finally, magically, it becomes the liquid medium for bird soup. The giblets and neck meat may be saved and used in hash or soup.

Ingredients

giblets

neck

6–7 cups water

- Place the giblets and neck into a 2-quart saucepan. Add the water and bring to a boil. Reduce the heat and cover. Simmer for 2 hours.

Makes about 6 cups.

HAM STOCK

Hams, like turkeys, can seem as endless as eternity. But eventually you get down to the bones. Sometimes they're cooked in the soup, sometimes converted into stock. Either way, they add splendid flavor to whatever's simmering. The following recipe involves roasting the bones before they're placed in water. It's quite possible, of course, to make ham stock simply by boiling. Roasting, however, intensifies the flavor and gives the stock a glorious red-brown color. Do remove as much of the fat as possible before placing the bones in the oven.

Variation: Use pork instead of ham. The meaty bones of a pork roast are most amenable to the treatment given below.

Ingredients

1 meaty ham bone (or pork bones)

½ cup red wine

10 cups water

- Place a rack in the center of the oven. Preheat to 500° Fahrenheit.

- Put the meaty bones in a small roasting pan. Roast on one side for 10 minutes. Turn and roast on the other side for 10 minutes. Remove the bones and place them in a stockpot.

- Pour off any fat from the roasting pan. Place the pan on top of the stove over high heat. Pour in the wine. Bring to a boil, scraping browned drippings from the bottom of the pan. Let the liquid reduce by half. Pour over the bones.

- Add water to cover the bones by 1 inch. Bring to a boil, then reduce the heat and simmer for 8 to 12 hours, occasionally skimming off fat and froth. Check the water level every 2 to 3 hours. Keep it 1 inch above the bones.

- Strain through cheesecloth or a fine sieve. Skim the fat. Let cool to room temperature, then refrigerate overnight.

- Remove any remaining fat and also the sediment settled out on the bottom. Use right away or freeze until needed.

Makes about 8 cups.

Seafood Stocks

Summers on the Carolina coast, we spend a perhaps inordinate amount of time fishing and crabbing in the wide and salty river Neuse, 75 feet from our front door. Spot and croaker, spotted seatrout, red drum, Spanish mackerel, bluefish, flounder, and more entangle themselves in our net, are brought ashore, and cleaned within 12 hours. We also haunt the local docks to get the freshest possible shrimp from a newly arrived trawler. Using fish and shrimp stocks to make soups from these marine creatures assures their delectability. And the stocks are easy to prepare.

Fish Stock

Fish stock is best made from fish frames, which consist of the head, the tail, and the bones between. We catch our own fish, of course, and freeze the frames for future use, but inlanders without our front-yard access to the ocean's bounty may order whole fish from seafood dealers. Two rules of thumb apply. First, use nonoily fish like red drum, red snapper, or rockfish for the stock. Second, use 2½ cups of water for each pound of fish bones. Some recipes for fish stock specify that it be simmered with vegetables and peppercorns. No, no, no! They're not one whit necessary, for onions and other goodies are added when the soup itself is cooked.

Ingredients

4 pounds fish heads and bones

10 cups water

• Place the fish pieces in a large stockpot and add water. (There should be enough to cover the fish. If not, add just a little more.) Bring to a boil, then reduce the heat and simmer for 4 hours.

• Cool to room temperature. Remove the fish pieces. Strain the stock through cheesecloth or a fine sieve. Use right away, refrigerate, or freeze.

Makes 8 cups.

Shrimp Stock

Some recipes for shrimp stock call for brewing it with a host of vegetables, herbs, and spices—onion, garlic, carrot, celery, basil, thyme, and even cloves. But all those things may be added when the stock becomes the basis for a soup containing this most succulent crustacean. In my view, simplicity wins out in the matter of using it for stock. Save the shells when you prepare shrimp for other dishes, and freeze them until you have enough. The resulting stock will be pale, almost luminous gold in color.

Ingredients

shells from 4 pounds of shrimp

10 cups water

4 peppercorns (optional)

• Place the shells in a large soup pot (no need to thaw them first). Cover with 10 cups of water. Bring to a boil. Reduce the heat and simmer for 30 minutes.

Makes about 7 cups.

Ah, stock! It's the beginning of soup's good music. And most stock is uncomplicated, taking only minutes to prepare, hours to simmer down, and another few minutes to cool and store. "Hours" may sound onerous, but while the cooking is under way, you're free to do almost anything else. The only requirement is to glance occasionally at the level of liquid in the pot and add more if needed.

With a great good homemade stock, you're well on your way to playing the good tune of *shloop, shloop, shloop.*

Chapter Seven
Companions

$\mathcal{S}$oup you can stand your spoon in needs little else to create a well-rounded, satisfying meal. Yet there are light touches that add flavor, color, and deliciousness to a soup-centered meal. Here are eight of my favorites.

Corn Bread

What goes best with pea or lentil soup? Corn bread, of course.

Cornmeal, its prime ingredient, has figured in American recipes since the Spanish explorers discovered that wonder of the New World, maize, which was a staple crop in many Indian settlements, along with squash and beans. Recipes found in the earliest American cookbook, *American Cookery*, call it "Indian meal." That cookbook, written by Amelia Simmons, a household servant, was published in 1796. And here's her recipe for "Johny Cake," a kissing cousin to corn bread:

> Scald 1 pint of milk and put to 3 pints of Indian meal, and half pint of flower—bake before the fire. Or scald two thirds of the Indian meal, or wet two thirds with boiling water, add salt, molasses and shortening, work up with cold water pretty stiff, and bake as above.

And ever since, American cookbooks from Mary Randolph's 1824 *Virginia Housewife* to *The Joy of Cooking* and Fanny Farmer's eponymous tome have featured breads made with cornmeal. Fortunately, we need not use a fire but have easy access to temperature-regulated ovens. We can also be sure of consistently good results. The following recipe was adapted from one that first appeared on a box of Quaker Corn Meal.

> **Variation:** Add 3 pods jalapeño pepper, seeded and finely diced, and ½ cup grated cheddar cheese. Bake as directed.

Ingredients

1 cup yellow cornmeal

1 cup flour

¼ cup sugar

4 teaspoons baking powder

¼ teaspoon salt

1 egg

1 cup milk

¼ cup soft butter or shortening

- Preheat the oven to 450° Fahrenheit.
- Stir together cornmeal, flour, sugar, baking powder, and salt. Add the egg, milk, and butter. Beat until smooth.
- Pour the batter into a lightly greased 8-inch-by-8-inch pan. Bake for 20 to 25 minutes, or until a toothpick inserted into the center comes out clean.

Makes 9 squares.

Saltwater Corn Cakes

The recipe comes from Sandy Taylor, who is also responsible for a luxurious Broccoli and Cheese Soup (page 6). She discovered and appropriated the corn cakes recipe when she lived in Tennessee. They were a popular item served at a Nero's, a famous barbecue place in Nashville. Alas, Nero's is no more. The recipe is preserved, however, in a battered spiral-bound cookbook, *What's Cooking at Oak Hill* (a school in Nashville). Sandy indulges in fond memories and honors Nero's every time that she stirs together cornmeal, salt, and water and deep-fries the little cakes in hot oil. Sandy's special instructions—not found in Oak Hill's cookbook—are given below in quotation marks.

She adds an economical note on freezing what you don't use:

- Fry the cakes for half the time specified. Let them cool; then place them in freezer bags. The next time you'd savor them, take however many you want from the bags and fry them in oil (though not to cover) for the other half of the time specified.

Ingredients

2 cups water

½ teaspoon salt

1¼–1½ cups yellow cornmeal

cooking oil

- Bring the water to a boil in a medium saucepan, reduce the heat to low, and gradually add the salt and meal. "If the mush seems too thick, add more hot water from the tap." Then refrigerate the mixture for 20 minutes.

- Shape mixture into balls about 1 inch in diameter, "the size of a golf ball"; then flatten them out.

- Put cooking oil, enough to cover the cakes by ½ inch, into a heavy skillet and heat over medium. When the oil is swirling and spitting a little, immerse the cakes and fry until golden brown, about 5 minutes. Turn them once while frying.

- "Serve them brushed with melted butter."

Makes 16 to 18 cakes.

Damper: An Australian Bread

This recipe is also Sandy Taylor's. In her kitchen, cookbooks, from fat and elegant to spiral bound and falling apart, are stacked on every counter, and on the inner doors of the cupboards that contain food, old and new recipes, clipped from newspapers and magazines, are taped. Damper is one of the latter, and from its yellowed appearance, it's been there for a long time. It means something special to Sandy, who first ate it when, in her unmarried younger days, she lived for four sweet years in Australia, where she worked as a marketing consultant for a computer magazine.

But *damper*—what kind of name is that? As might be expected, given the continent on which the name has landed upon a kind of unleavened bread, it's British. In this case and in general, it refers to something that can dampen—take the edge off—hunger. And that it does. Use lots of butter, and don't forget to dip it in the soup. It goes particularly well with soups that feature meat.

Ingredients

5½ tablespoons butter

3 cups self-rising flour

½ cup milk

½ cup water

- Preheat the oven to 425° Fahrenheit.

- Cut the butter into the flour with a pastry blender until crumbly. Add the milk and water, stirring until the dry ingredients are moistened.

- Turn the dough out onto a lightly floured surface. With moistened hands, knead it three or four times. Shape dough into a 7-inch circle and place it on a baking sheet that has been coated with cooking spray. Cut ½-inch-deep X across the top of the dough. Lightly coat the dough with cooking spray.

- Bake for 25 to 28 minutes, or until lightly browned.

Serves 8.

Just Plain Muffins

For decades—since May, 1968, to be exact—this recipe has been a household favorite. I first met it in *Golden Magazine*, to which one of my children subscribed. Bleached flour, unbleached flour, or wheat flour, it's always simple and fail-safe. To fancify it:

- Fill muffin cups half full of batter. Drop 1 teaspoon of jelly—strawberry, grape, your choice—in the center of the batter. Add more batter to fill cups two-thirds full.

Serve the muffins with bean soups and meaty soups like Beef Soup with Vegetables (page 93).

Ingredients

2 cups flour

¼ cup sugar

1 tablespoon baking powder

1 teaspoon salt

1 egg

1 cup milk

¼ cup vegetable oil

- Preheat the oven to 400˚ Fahrenheit.

- In a large bowl, stir together the flour, sugar, baking powder, and salt. Make a well in the center of the mixture.

- In another bowl, beat the egg lightly with a fork. Stir in the milk and oil.

- Pour the egg mixture all at once into the well in the flour mixture. Stir just until the flour is moistened. The batter will be slightly lumpy.

- Grease the bottoms of 12 medium-sized muffin cups. Fill the cups two-thirds full.

- Bake for 20 to 25 minutes, or until golden brown.

Makes 12 muffins.

Pan Relleno

Pan relleno is Spanish for "stuffed bread." Where this recipe came from, and when, I cannot recall. The yellowed card in my recipe file attributes it to Anonymous. It's easy to make and is a splendid companion for any minestrone.

Ingredients

1 long loaf French bread

1 cup grated cheddar cheese

½ cup finely diced onion

¼ cup green olives, chopped

¼ teaspoon dried oregano

3 tablespoons olive oil

1 tablespoon vinegar

• Preheat the oven to 350° Fahrenheit.

• Slice the entire loaf of French bread in half lengthwise and scoop out some of its soft insides. Mix the bread you've removed with the cheese, onion, olives, oregano, oil, and vinegar. Fill the loaf with this mixture, replace the top, and wrap in foil.

• Bake for 20 minutes, or until well heated.

Serves at least 8.

Spätzle: German Egg Dumplings

Spätzle (pronounced SHPATES-leh) is German for "little sparrow." Along with the making of lentil soup, my first husband insisted that I learn also to make these egg dumplings, which are traditionally cooked in that particular "peasant food." They are added to soup for the last 20 minutes of cooking. Make sure that there's enough liquid in the soup pot for them to float in. After the dough is added to the soup, they'll rise to the surface as they cook.

Ingredients

1 egg

¾ cup flour

¼ cup water

½ teaspoon salt

¼ teaspoon baking powder

• Beat the egg lightly in a small bowl. Add the other ingredients and mix them thoroughly with the egg.

• Drop small bits of batter into the simmering soup with a flatware tea-spoon. The batter will slide more easily off a spoon that has been dipped into the soup. Cover the soup and simmer the *Spätzle* for 20 minutes. Serve immediately.

Potato Dumplings

I've met recipes for potato dumplings that end in disaster: They do not dumple, cooking in discrete balls, but fall apart and float like foam atop the soup. But this recipe is well-nigh immune to failure. Use it in Harvest Minestrone (page 43); in Hearty Tuscan Minestrone, instead of tortelloni or gnocchi (page 41); or in Chicken and Pasta Soup instead of the pasta (page 119). I prefer to cook and mash potatoes especially for the occasion rather than using leftovers. The dumplings are plopped into the soup 10 minutes before serving.

Several tasty transformations may be worked on the basic recipe:

- When you mash the potatoes, add 1 tablespoon minced onion flakes.
- Or, when you make the dough, add 1 tablespoon chopped fresh parsley or 1 teaspoon chopped fresh dill (more of the latter, if you really like dill).
- When you make the dough balls, form each one around a crouton.

Ingredients

1½ cups mashed potatoes

1 teaspoon salt

1 egg

½ cup flour

- Combine the potatoes, salt, egg, and flour. With moistened hands, roll the dough into 1-inch balls.

- Drop the dumplings into the soup. Cook for 10 minutes. Serve.

Makes about 16 to 18 dumplings.

Cheese Bread

The recipe for cheese bread came my way long ago from my daughter Elisabeth, who has a way with both yeasted and unyeasted breads. I have little success with the former, but this one is fail-safe, even for a bread burner like me. And, oh, it is scrumptiously buttery. Cheddar cheese may be used instead of Swiss. Serve it with soups made from beans and other legumes.

Ingredients

⅔ cup water

½ cup butter, cut into pieces

⅔ cup flour

¼ teaspoon salt

3 large eggs

½ cup Swiss cheese, shredded

- Preheat the oven to 400° Fahrenheit.

- Bring the water and butter to a rolling boil in a medium saucepan. Remove from the heat and immediately add the flour and salt all at once. Beat with a wooden spoon until blended. Return to the heat and beat vigorously until the dough balls up and leaves the sides of the pan, about 1 minute. Reduce the heat to low and cook for 5 minutes.

- Beat in the eggs, one at a time, until the batter is glossy. Blend in the cheese thoroughly.

- Dampen a shallow baking pan with cold water. Drop dough in large dollops onto the pan to form a ring, with the sides of the dollops touching.

- Bake for 30 minutes, until puffed and golden brown. Remove from the oven and loosen immediately from the pan with a spatula. The cheese bread will stick a little.

Serves 6.

May your kitchen be fragrant with stocks and broths, herbs and spices, and, always, the inimitable aromas of onions and garlic. I wish you *bon appétit* and much good music as you *shloop, shloop, shloop.*

INDEX